A World of Illusions

A Wake-Up Call and the Search for the Truth

Paola Knecht

Knecht Publishing

To my beloved children

Contents

Publisher: Knecht Publishing

ISBN: 978-3-033-10039-8

Edition: Paul Blane & Skip Press

Cover Illustration: David Colón

Cover Design: David Colón

Disclaimer

Introduction

R. Buckminister Fuller, American architect, inventor of the geodesic dome, second World President of Mensa International, and author of more than 30 books, once said this: "99.999% of what affects our reality will be undetectable by our senses. Man must learn to think for himself, rather than follow blindly what he has been taught."

This book reflects that sentiment precisely. My purpose is writing it is to invite you to develop a critical mind about world events today and join a collective awakening which is so crucial in our rapidly evolving times.

Our world today has been dominated by fear and threats to our very survival. The younger ones among us are constantly reminded of all the dangers that threaten to consume us all. Human misery and suffering threatens to be our main contribution to history. From the very moment we are born, detached from our mother's umbilical cord and taken away from her by foreign hands in an abrupt way, we begin our existence in a struggle, entering this world in a state of distress.

The nostalgia that envelops so many of the Baby Boomer generation today might well stem from a longing to get back to what we lost after months of comfort in our mother's womb. And so it is with each generation, all seeking nourishment, tranquility, intimate connection, and an innate conviction that we are protected and loved.

In our attempt to regain that lost paradise of gestation, we can become obsessed with regaining a sense of security, even if for only a brief moment. The problem with that longing is that we often look in the wrong places. We learn, all too often, that most things that society promises will bring us happiness never really live up to expectations. The moral compass that defines our Western societies seems to spin toward decadence; people move away from patriotism, religion, and family values, while falling prey to ideologies that are the antithesis of those traditions. Then we find that intolerance, violence, anti-family agendas, and an overall lack of a moral compass lead us to a spiral into nowhere.

This shift in values has been a process so gradual it escaped the notice of most people in Western society. As has been the case throughout history, daily life for most of us is a busy struggle for survival. It is hard to pay attention to how our society transforms itself over the decades. To most of us, the "Zeitgeist" (the spirit of our times) is a wave ridden by humanity with too few examining its source.

What if this were not the case? What if we learned that the Zeitgeist is orchestrated by unknown "puppet masters" and we are purposely kept ignorant of the guiding societal forces in our life?

If this is so, do we perpetuate our own crisis and misery? Do we accept "reality" too easily? Governments, global institutions, and celebrities, together with the mainstream media, tell us over and over that climate change is our fault, that wars are created by us, that the poor are poor because they deserve it. We are told that "third-world countries" are simply a lower class of people than those populating "first-world countries."

Must we accept the fate preached to us, forever remaining slaves of our own wrongdoing? Do we truly save ourselves by paying carbon taxes, reducing meat consumption, or buying impossibly expensive electric cars? All of these presented solutions merely shift the problems rather than mitigate them. And then we are told that we must learn to self-manage our crises by stay happily confined in "15-minute cities."

My purpose with this book is to provide you with a critical analysis of the latest world events and explain how my understanding of reality completely shifted as I awoke to a better reality.

In the first section, I reference the recent health crisis, social constructs, and accelerated developments in technology. I reflect on how a shift from traditional understandings have been altered by what we have been told about topics like health, nutrition, sex, and family values. "Progressive" ideas have been shown to be based on false and even dangerous premises about our physical and mental health.

An increased use of social media has only exacerbated the problems. Instead of bringing us closer and providing us with access to more information as initially assumed, we have become more isolated and narrow-minded in a few short decades. Social media was sold to us as a marvelous tool to bring the world into the next level of communication. In some ways it did, but it also brought out the worst in too many of us and put our shortcomings on permanent display for the world.

In the second section of my book, I describe how some toxic ideologies are causing a profound division in societies, a malaise that has been spreading with enormous speed in recent times. I describe how ideologies like white supremacism, gender equality and transgender movements, political correctness, climate change, overpopulation, and globalization are provoking a profound division in all our human affairs and are only serving to increase worldwide levels of violence, poverty, and social unrest.

In the last section, I invite you to initiate your own

search for truth so that you can arrive at your unique conclusion regarding the state of the world and how we can revive what made our societies great. I invite you to return with me to a life of common sense, critical thinking, true moral virtues, and the real transcendence of humanity through coming back to our Source, the divine power of God.

An important step toward gaining back your critical thinking and common sense is to recognize that we have been lied to and manipulated at all levels our whole life. All erroneous ideologies come from external and powerful sources that have a great ability to manipulate reality. We all can, however, choose to be free. You can choose to get out of the toxic grid of media and become a critical thinker, a true master of your own body and soul.

Everything I expose in this book comes from my own personal research and perspective about the state of the world. I do not intend to convince you that you should necessarily come to the same conclusions that I did, or that my truth is the only truth. My intention is to reveal my own path in realizing how a world that I treasured was robbed from us. I am working now for a world where we stop losing our sovereignty and regain our dignity and independence as human beings.

We are living in a time when "opinions" are sent forth at great speed. Both true information and misinformation can spread almost instantaneously around the planet. This can be troublesome, because people nowadays tend to believe that they "understand reality" simply by listening to their personal choices of media, which could be a news source or any influencer on the Internet.

As adults, we learn that opinions are not the same as knowledge. In the 4th century, Aristotle claimed that knowledge is an objective necessity, and that it requires the use of our thought processes to follow facts and events, make logical connections, and arrive at causal conclusions.

Accordingly, knowledge requires proper research and a rigorous thought process. With these standards in mind, I want to share the results of my own investigative journey and hopefully help you with your own.

I sincerely hope that you join our revolution, which is an evolution of awakening souls. If that sounds like something you've been yearning for, keep reading. Let me take you on a bumpy, but ultimately reassuring and revealing ride to a destination where you will arrive in much better control of your environment and life.

Part One
A World Made By Illusions

1. What We Learned About Health Is Wrong

THERE is no area in our lives where I feel we have been so malignantly misinformed about than in the topic of health. Let me give you some examples.

In the 21st century, a symbol seen on almost all first responder vehicles is a caduceus. A winged staff encircled by twin serpents that was carried by Hermes, messenger of the gods in Greek mythology, and also by Hermes Trismegistus in Greco-Egyptian mythology. Doctors and pharmaceutical providers now serve as our mythological equivalent in the West, presented as bringers of godlike health solutions mere humans can barely understand. If you doubt this, take the time to watch any of a myriad of TV pharmaceutical ads of products with made-up names and scenes of happy people as an announcer in the background hurriedly recites a myriad of possible side effects that are possible. Illusion is created, and people go along.

The "official" symbolism of the caduceus enforces a disassociation and distrust of our own sensations and intuition about our personal health. We have learned to give all authority over our well-being to strangers who display this symbol and we allow them to judge our health and our capability to remain healthy.

Meanwhile, natural remedies with fresh ingredients coming from our very soil and water, that have been tried and tested by our ancestors over thousands of years, are belittled and often labelled as "alternative medicine" - alluding to non-scientific methods of healing. Practices that have been ingrained in cultures for millennia, like Ayurveda in India, or traditional Chinese medicine, are often not included in most health care systems in the West.

Switzerland, for example, only officially included any "alternative medicine" in health care insurance coverage as late as 2021.[1]

Why is it that we distrust natural remedies which have successfully existed for the majority of our history? Why do we implicitly believe so much in the "science" which has taken a rather mechanistic approach, especially since the second world war? Western medicine is fundamentally based on the idea that the body resembles a machine. The brain is regarded as the master, the nerves are the messenger wires, and the organs the obedient servants. Somewhere beyond that is a sort of 'consciousness' or soul that coexists with the body. The spiritual elemental of health, however, has been downplayed in medicine for decades, since the beginning of the 20th century.

Conventional or traditional medicine, known as "allopathic" medicine, is where healthcare professionals use a range of standardized treatments to treat infection, illness, and disease. The word comes from the Greek *alios* meaning "opposite" combined with *pathos* meaning "to suffer." Coined by German physician Samuel Hahnemann in the 1800s, allopathy means using the opposite of a symptom to cure it, like a laxative to solve constipation. Oddly enough, Dr. Hahnemann became interested in ancient health principles of treating "like with like" and pursued that, becoming known as the founder of homeopathy.

An allopathic view neglects the holistic law of other approaches that have sustained us throughout history and neglects to account for countless generations of accumulated wisdom, where the organs cooperate harmoniously and not in a hierarchical order. Prominent scientists, like the Austrian doctor Wilhem Reich,[2] who challenged the mechanistic view of man, argue that the individual organs are like independent beings, bestowed with their own sensations and functions.

Reich is one of the fathers of orgonomy, a relatively new field of study that specializes in understanding the function of orgastic plasma pulsations, which is the energy released through the excitation stage in a living organism. "Orgone" is the name Reich gave to the energy pulsation he observed while doing his research; he called it "the energy from which all nature is created." In other words, the creative force in nature. The principles to which orgone energy operates have these characteristics:

1. it is mass-free and has no inertia,
2. it is universal,
3. it is the medium for electromagnetic and gravitational activity, and
4. it is that from which matter is created.

Reich found enough evidence through his many years of research to conclude that each organ has its own mode of expression, its own specific language. Each organ reacts to stimuli in its own specific way: for example, the heart's expression is a change in heartbeat, the gland secretes, the eye can change visual impressions, and so on.

By Reich's estimation, precise expressive language belongs to each individual organ, and it is not a function of any center in the nervous system. In his orgonotic research, Reich found a gap in humanity's understanding of the nature of man and our relationship with the environment. He argued that, for millennia, man had neglected the role that sensations play in the overall picture of health and well-being.

An Eastern corollary of this sentiment might be seen in the energy centers known as chakras in Ayurvedic medicine in India. Arranged in a column along the spinal cord, upward from its base to the top of the head, there is a chakra at the base, the abdomen, the heart, the throat, and the crown of the head.

Reich compared different human character structures and observed that when you study the nature of man through a character structure that is armored, rigid and mechanistic (i.e., excluding the study of any single body sensation), this produces mechanistic tools and forms a mechanistic conception of nature. When an "armored" person experiences orgonotic body excitation, despite his rigid way of thinking, he does not really understand it, and doing so becomes a mystic man.

Mysticism is the "spiritual" path that creates a supernatural idea about the world and how it operates. Reich argued that neither the "mechanistic" nor the "mystical" views of the world have served humanity, and in fact, this is the middle point of the eternal battle between "machines" and "gods."

When Reich further explored the field of sensations, he realized that his discovery transcended the civilization frameworks of the "mechanical-mystical" nature to enter into the unknown world of sensations, which he called the orgonomic functionalism. That is, the vital expression of an animal that is "unarmored" and reacts to the stimuli of nature. Hence, sensations are the natural and direct tools we have to interact and understand nature.

Eccles and Popper, in their book *The Self and Its Brain*,[3] also criticize what they call "Radical materialism" or radical physicalism, which is a reductionist view of the world that simplifies everything into basic processes and relationships. They argue that although it is an attractive method because it offers simple theories, it is at the same time totally contradictory to nature, because the radical physicalist must adopt radical behavior to sustain the theory, which means; the thoughts, actions, and words must be radically simplified as well, which is unattainable due to our own functional evolving nature.

As you can see, medicine has never been completely fixed in place with all solutions worked out for all humankind. Instead, faces that are often self-interested try to dominate other theories.

The contrary to the simplification of the radical materialism is what Eccles and Popper called the "philosophical reduction," which is characterized by an attempt to attribute what is unknown to the intervention of higher powers. There's Hermes and his caduceus again, and we revisit the battle between the machines and the gods discussed by Reich.

The human animal can only understand his or her place in the world by thinking and acting in line with how nature works. Functional thinking does not tolerate static conditions. All natural processes are in motion, in flux. Everything that is alive in nature is in constant movement to survive, even if the movements are happening at a microscopical level inside a living body.

The remedies that we find at pharmacies claiming to cure a specific malady in a specific area of the body are based on a mechanistic thinking of the body. In reality, a specific substance intake will have an impact on the body as a whole, often with secondary effects that were not expected. (The possible effects are warned about in the background of pharmaceutical commercials.) Reich warned us about this mechanistic approach and claimed that "A mechanistic civilization is a deviation from the law of nature; even more, it is a perversion of nature, an extremely dangerous variant".[4]

The belief that our own body is the sum of its individual, isolated parts disconnects us from our real nature. We are interconnected at all levels in our body, mind, and soul. The sensations we feel in our bodies have a direct impact on our emotions, and our emotions are of bio-energetic nature. It follows that we as individuals are not a "sum of body parts plus a soul."

So, what keeps our organs working harmoniously? What elusive, all-powerful force is intervening in all living matter?

These questions inspired prominent scientists like Reich in their quest to find an answer, which he did by discovering the orgonomic energy stream. It is universally existing, all permeating, and the origin of all energy and matter that fills up our visible and invisible space. When these orgonotic energy streams attract each other by an impulse mechanism, they can merge using superimposition, which is a bio-energetic involuntary action, a force that cannot be stopped consciously by us, just as we cannot stop a heartbeat or reactively blinking our eyes, unless there is a forceful intervention that causes death.

This energy operates by the common functional principle of life and exists in all nature. Reich could prove the existence of these energies and their operating principle and found the evidence of similar patterns of behavior of the energy streams in hurricanes, the aurora borealis, and photosynthesis, among other natural processes. His was a worldview that encompassed all of nature and living creatures.

Weaponization of the functional orgasm

AS HUMANS, we are supposed to feel connected to our nature and to the world, and one of the obvious processes where it is manifested is in the way we reproduce. Society has weaponized the orgasm and the superimposition of the genital embrace either by making it a taboo, or by misusing it to the point of considering it as pornographic, shameful, or just plain morbid.

With all this, we have buried the possibility of using this our life force energy stream as a resource to repair our health and rediscover our intimate connection with nature in true freedom. It is through this "armor" in stable sexual energy that societies have separated themselves from the rest of the living.

In the early 1930s, Reich made three major discoveries which could change the view we have about orgasms and our relationship with the environment forever. He found out that the libido is a flow of real energy; that the orgasm acts as a regulator of this flow of energy, and that the muscular rigidity experienced by stress and repression blocks this flow of energy and prevents its proper regulation. He also discovered that this energy when blocked is the main cause of stifled perceptions and emotions, which often end up developing as neurosis in individuals. This was also reported in the works of Freud and Jung. [5,6]

The theory of orgonotic energy has been severely criticized and downgraded to "pseudo-science" to the point that if you try to research it on Google, you will mostly get information that advocates downgrading Reich's discovery.

That's the reason you have probably never heard of Wilhelm Reich, nor about orgonomic energy in a positive light. Back in the 1950s, Reich gained a lot of popularity when he started to commercialize his latest invention, the orgone accumulator[7] and many patients started to report a gradual recovery from their neurosis or even cancer.

When the FDA (U.S. Food and Drug Administration) found out about Reich's devices, they issued an injunction against him, claiming that he violated the FDA's acts by delivering "misbranded and adulterated" devices for commercial purposes which are sustained in "non existent claims."

Then the FDA demanded the destruction of all the available machines. Finally, Reich was prosecuted by the FBI and eventually died in prison in 1957. Why would the FBI treat a scientist like Reich as a criminal, a man who intended to cure people from neurosis and even cancer using simple natural elements? Who was it that truly felt threatened by Reich?

Disconnection from nature equals disease

HUMANITY needs to gain back that connection to nature that we lost somewhere on the way. With so much progress and technological advancements we began, little by little, to separate ourselves from nature in so many ways: first, by building urban cities with few green areas, then replacing natural food with industrial processed food; and by closing our children in four walls to learn about the world during their primordial childhood years, instead of letting them wander free in nature. Even the essential sense of touch we used to enjoy, with our bare feet on sand, soil, and grass was lost to too many souls. Plastic and synthetic materials replaced the leather in our shoes. Artificial substitutes replaced natural Earth connections for people worldwide.

The result of this systemic separation from Nature has been quite alarming: even if we are told that we are living longer than our ancestors, we are not necessarily living *better* or *healthier*. Today, the number of chronic sickness cases has skyrocketed like never before. Alzheimer's, cancer, dementia, diabetes, autism, and many other conditions which were relatively non-existent just half a century ago are prevalent. Such maladies have become the norm of adult life in Western societies; and sadly, not only with adults, but in the last decades such health issues have been extended to far too many young people.

45% of Americans have at least one chronic disease. In fact, chronic diseases are the leading cause of death and disability in the United States.

Why is it going on? How can it be that we spend billions of dollars on healthcare while our health is getting worse? In 2020, for example, the United States reached the whopping amount of 4.1 trillion dollars in healthcare spending, which is something like 12,500 dollars per person![8] Isn't that insane?

We are sicker than ever. Despite having an amazingly huge healthcare industry dominated by the so called "big pharma" and the trillions and trillions spent on governmental healthcare policies, NGOs, philanthropic institutions, health insurances and so on, the reality is that our life expectancy is declining and our quality of life is decreasing, thanks to the multiple degenerative "modern" diseases that attack our immune systems.

It took a while for me to accept the harsh reality that I have been lied to my whole life about what healthcare really means. When I realized that the more I fell into the "science," the further I am taken away from common sense and observable natural laws of the living, I came to the realization that something was very wrong. Not just wrong in a naïve way; something was profoundly wrong in our human interaction and our level of consciousness and understanding of effective health measures.

Are we so easy to manipulate that we will respond to a drug ad and ask a health professional to give it to us? Apart from the obvious greediness and hunger for power that drive big pharma and healthcare systems, what is the underlying motive to keep the populations dependent on expensive healthcare schemes and expensive treatments for the rest of their lives?

When did we lose trust in natural remedies that are free and abundant? When did we relinquish our inner knowledge of how life and nature works, and give our trust to the so-called "experts" that appear on TV? These people often have no clue about your best health nor the health of others and are sponsored by giant institutions run by executives who often seem anonymous. What is the real purpose of these experts, and why should we trust them? You will tell me that it is because they "know" more than you, and because they are on TV, so they must be telling the truth, because the media would never lie to us, we good citizens, we well-intentioned, regular people who pay the taxes on time. Yeah, right...Right?

2. We Are What We Eat, But What Are We Eating?

MOST PEOPLE in the world today are undernourished. Wait, what? I mean, come on. This cannot be true. How can that be if in nearly every city of the world there are supermarkets filled up with all kinds of food? It could even be argued that we even have too much food. We live in a world of abundance and overproduction.

At first sight, I would agree with these thoughts. It seems on the surface that we have an excess amount of food in major Western cities, although poorly distributed. But let's think it through. What does it mean to be well-nourished? You would surely agree that it's true to say that a nourished individual is someone who eats wholesome, healthy and delicious food that fills them up with all the energy and nutrients they need. Not enough people, however, have a good enough understanding of nutrition. Thankfully, there are movements to improve this situation.

Let's take a look at the food available in a typical supermarket. Your local store will most likely will be a branded, well-known retail shop if you live in a big city. Let's take Walmart, for example, or even my local shop Migros, a popular food supermarket chain in Switzerland.

At first sight, the supermarket is filled with food. Around 80% of what is offered in the store comes in a sort of package. When you walk through the different aisles you will find many varieties of branded cereals, pasta, yogurt, processed cookies and pastries, milk, and so on.

How blessed we are that we are able to have so much abundance and variety of food, most people think.

In the 'fresh section' you have the fresh fruits and vegetables. Maybe, if we are lucky, we can buy three to four different varieties of apple, a banana or some potatoes. If I want an exotic fruit like a mango in Switzerland, however, I have to conform with maybe only one imported variety.

Yes, there is a lot of food, healthy and nutritious food available... right? Well, that was my belief until I became more skeptical about the real meaning of variety and diversity in food. My naïve view of food and nutrition basically fell apart the moment I learned from real food scientists like Vandana Shiva. She is working to defend against the real threat to agriculture, the destruction of small, diversified local farms in lieu of "modern agriculture," which is based on monocultures of genetically modified crops.

Shiva argues that the real problem of agriculture today is the controlled destruction of small *pluricultural* farms, mainly run by rural women who have been the real farmers for thousands of years, until only some decades ago. Women were traditionally the real and original food producers and the main pillar in the so-called food supply chain, until big corporations stole their seeds and soil and took control.

To understand how this shift has affected the real and sustainable agricultural practices, Shiva uses the example of several communities in India where you can still find diverse home garden agriculture that is organized and maintained by women.

In one community in Bengal, for example, there are more than 200 species of rice field varieties still being harvested by women. In Nigeria, women typically plant 18 to 57 different plant species in their home gardens to feed their families. All these practices are vanishing completely with the interference of "scientific" male dominated practices, and the introduction of the practice of monoculture, which involves planting limited varieties in mass quantities under the premise of feeding the population.

The introduction of monocultural farms is only made possible by the use of chemical "technologies" like fertilizers and pesticides and by consuming more land and water for huge irrigation systems. Although the big agrotech companies try to convince us that these practices as "progress in the favor of feeding the population," in reality they are causing three main effects. This "progress" produces chronic contamination of the soil and water, the transfer of control of food production from local and national levels to global corporations, and a real problem of malnutrition, hunger, and inequality.

Let's take a look at why. Agriculture has been around for thousands and thousands of years, since well before any modern technological development ever existed. Before we relied on modern technology, humanity used to eat more than 80,000 edible plants. Out of those, around 3,000 were being harvested continuously. In today's world, global agricultural corporations are mainly mass producing eight crops[1] (with the help of genetic engineering) to feed more than 75% of the world population and getting smaller.[2]

The limitation of the variety of crops we can consume also prevent us from getting the nutrients of all the other varieties we cannot consume anymore, and this leads to malnutrition. Also, with the number of fertilizers spread in the crops and in the soil, we end up consuming more chemicals than real nutrients, something we barely think about when we get our products from the supermarket.

We have been told for many decades now that we are rich in food, that we have more than enough to cover our needs, but is that really true? Will a box of packaged cereal feed me better than fresh, organic vegetables? Very unlikely, and in feeding children there are even more nuances. This came up in the 2024 American election, when Robert F. Kennedy Jr., nephew of the late President John F. Kennedy, posited that in the U.S., the cereal Froot Loops had a great many more ingredients than the Canadian version. The U.S. cereal had food flavorings and colorings that included red 40, yellow 5, blue 1, and yellow 6. Canadian Froot Loops, in contrast, were flavored with concentrated carrot juice, annatto turmeric, concentrated watermelon juice, concentrated blueberry juice, concentrated huito juice, and stevia leaf extract.

Fresh food is becoming an upstream luxury to people, and almost inaccessible to the poor. The irony, is that in third world countries, packaged and industrialized foods are being sold as the food of the rich, modern and handy. In actuality, rich people eat fresh foods, while the poor are being lied to and economically forced to buy processed and packaged foods.

Of course, the media plays a big role in how they sell us trashy food with, once again, sophisticated TV commercials and millions spent on PR campaigns. There is no doubt they have been very successful in selling the illusion of being cool by consuming fast food and drinking soft drinks and energy drink to mainstream populations. This must change, for optimum health.

How highly industrialized food is destroying our lives

WHO DOESN'T love a delicious pizza, with a crusty base, and double mozzarella cheese? Which child would resist not grabbing those colorful and attractive candy bags that have funny images and their favorite cartoon heroes strategically positioned to reach kids in supermarket stores? And how about Halloween? In the U.S., candies to kids are a parent's nightmare and a dentist's delight.

Candies are a sinister invention. They are often targeted at the most vulnerable of our kind, which are small kids and babies. We, as ignorant parents, think that giving some candy to our child will make them happy. You can see how the vibrant colors and sweet smells make your little one salivate. You give it to her as a 'compensation', a reward for doing something right for Papa and Mama.

Too few people take a look at the dark side of that innocent act. It turns out the lollipop is mainly made with sugar and corn syrup. Sugar has been proven to be highly addictive. Some researchers even suggest the addiction level is eight times higher than cocaine... that's right... eight times! [3] If it represents a big challenge to keep control of addictions for an adult, imagine what sugar does to the brain of a two-year-old toddler!

Kids love candies. Big food manufacturers know it and specifically target young ones as the main consumers of this questionable product. Who hasn't surrendered to buying that little chocolate bar displayed in all its splendor right in front of the check-out, especially if your child starts to cry, and you want to find a quick solution to silence them?

In this world of illusions, we need to look a little more closely.

Not only is sugar bad in the short term, but it can also cause problems in the long term, like immune system suppression, degenerative diseases, increased risk of diabetes, attention deficit disorder, among many others. [4] It goes without saying that too much sugar consumption is also related to accelerated tooth decay, [5] cardiovascular diseases, liver inflammation... the list could go on for a long while. A crusade against high fructose corn syrup in sodas has gone on for years now, so much so that, when discussing what Robert F. Kennedy Jr. might do in a healthcare office in the

U.S. federal government, he spoke of making soda bottlers use less dangerous cane syrup to sweeten drinks.

Despite knowing all this, some parents still allow their kids to drink sugary drinks, industrialized juices, flavored milk products, eat sweets, fast food like pizzas and hot dogs... Common sense would tell us that those are the last foods you want to give to your children. Nevertheless, we do it. I believe the behavioral dissonance between acting toward what common sense tells you versus what you actually do has a lot to do with the amount of influence you get in the environment. A backlash against trust in medicos after COVID has resulted in an increased interest in self-governed health, but there are great leaps necessary in improvement.

If you are confronted every day with TV commercials, influencers, newspaper publications, local events, and we are also reassured by how they sell these foods virtually everywhere, your awareness of the dangers of consumption do not trigger any alarms. You might think: is it really bad to drink Coca-Cola, or get the box of cereals with chocolate, if I can buy them anywhere and they are so heavily promoted? We believe too much in the wonderful commercials and ads, of happy, healthy children enjoying a delicious ice cream, or the Happy Meal from McDonald's, with a toy surprise included! What can be so wrong about that?

Companies like McDonald's have made huge advances in their marketing strategies targeting younger populations in countries like Brazil, where until recently, they sent their trademark clown Ronald McDonald to schools, nurseries and kindergartens to entertain the kids[6] in an effort to turn them into consumers. Although such practices have been banned in many schools, the company still targets youth in low to middle income countries.

According to recent research conducted by BMJ[7], McDonald's social media presence promoting their products is more active in middle to low income as compared to high income countries. In fact, they found that the social media posts were more child friendly and contained more product promotions in lower income countries than in wealthier ones.

This leaves me with the question, why? Why would McDonald's run a different campaign strategy targeting young children in more vulnerable countries to their strategy in richer ones? What is the interest behind promoting the worst quality of food to the most vulnerable? Why would such a globally renowned company be interested in destroying kids' strong immune systems? In exchange for steady sales? Could it be that simple and dire?

I have certainly become more skeptical about the good intentions of the "big food industry" over the last few years. I always had some awareness that highly processed food is less healthy than fresh food, but when it comes to looking for the right choice, if one neglects your own intuition, you can be easily misled by media messages.

Ads for highly processed food often portray happy and healthy people doing exercise such as football stars drinking Coca-Cola before the Champions League tournament, high level athletes drinking Gatorade before their competition to "boost energy," or kids having a highly processed sugary cereal in the morning before going to school. All these images playing in your mind directly or indirectly send you the signal that ingesting the foods depicted is completely normal, and if they are so popular and seen everywhere, it must be because it is good, no?

It is no surprise by now to know that humanity is suffering from increasing chronic diseases and lower life expectancy as we advance on our path to "progress." We already discussed how big pharma companies have been profiting from our ignorance about how our body works, and how ignoring simple laws of nature make us target to all sorts of manipulations to make us believe that we do not have any power whatsoever to keep ourselves healthy and that "science" knows better.

It seems clear that following the advice of medical experts about consuming all sorts of synthetic, chemical medication and eating synthetic, processed food is not really taking us far in terms of keeping us healthy and striving.

What can we do about it? I believe the first step is to become skeptical and question everything you see and hear. You can trust if you wish but verify. The point is not to become paranoid and stop eating anything packaged, but at least, when you choose consciously, you have the power to think twice and modify certain consumption behaviors that seemed harmless at the beginning, but which really do have an adverse effect on your life.

The low-fat diet fallacy

DO YOU REMEMBER how people used to tell you that eggs, butter and cheese are high in cholesterol, and therefore it would be unthinkable to eat them in big quantities if you don't want to suffer from heart attacks, obesity and cardiovascular diseases? Not to mention the high amount of toxins that red meat contains and that we would be better off moving towards a diet more abundantly filled with veggies and cereals.

I was mostly following that advice, and I believed that cholesterol was a bad thing to be avoided in order to maintain a good weight and keep healthy. However, I realized that every time I moved to a low-fat diet, I struggled more to actually lose weight and suffered from difficulties maintaining mental sharpness.

I tried a lot of things along the way: I tried to be vegetarian during the week, and reduced consumption of red meats, eggs and cheese during the weekends. To make up for the loss, I consumed more pastas and cereals as an additional source of energy. The results after a couple of weeks were no better. I often felt hungry, and despite eating more vegetables, fruits and cereals, I still felt a certain lack of energy. My weight was not improving, and I also experienced some anxiety and an unexplainable feeling of having blurry thoughts.

It was not until I discovered Dr. David Perlmutter and his work on linking neurological diseases with the consumption of high-carb diets that I started questioning if the wholegrain cereals, breads and pastas that I was consuming were part of the problem.

In his book *Grain Brain -The Surprising Truth about Wheat, Carbs and Sugar*[8], Dr. Perlmutter argues that the killer ingredient in modern food manufacturing today is the gluten that comes from highly processed grains. The gluten that we consume in those industrialized foods is less tolerable for the human body than the natural gluten that was contained in food decades ago.

More problematic is when we combine gluten with sugar and other added carbohydrates; together they create an inflammatory bomb in our bodies, which also eventually affects our brain. Dr. Perlmutter makes his case and proves how a high-carb-based diet combined with a low-fat and low cholesterol regime can be very dangerous, and the main trigger to serious degenerative diseases such as Alzheimer's, schizophrenia, seizures, and even cardiac arrests. If you want to know more about the topic and also learn how to introduce high cholesterol, high (good) fats into your diet, I strongly recommend getting his book.

The point I want to make here is that for most of my whole life, I felt lied to by the food industry and medical establishments that demonized cholesterol and promoted it as the villain of the story; when in reality the natural cholesterol (HDL) is a life-essential substance, critical in keeping us healthy and alive. Cholesterol is the most important construction material of most of our hormones. The cell walls of our body are actually built with cholesterol, and it's the vital substance that keep ATP cells, responsible for storing energy, working optimally.

Something not many people know is that our bodies naturally produce cholesterol in the liver. To get additional support, our bodies can get it from meats, eggs, and healthy fats like olives, coconut oils, fish and nuts. The more healthy cholesterol that is produced, the lower the chances of getting cardiovascular diseases. I did the test myself and started consuming more healthy fats and reduced my amount of cereal intake and was amazed by the results.

I finally observed a sustained loss of weight, general increase in my energy levels, and an improved capability to keep myself focused on difficult tasks. Of course, it is worthwhile to consult your local doctor or nutritionist and review your own personal health situation before making any extreme dietary changes to ensure that you do not put yourself at risk.

As a final note: the key to a healthy and happy life is to respect our genome and understand that fat and not carbohydrates are the preferred fuel of human metabolism and has been so since the beginning of civilization.

3. Chronicles Of A Pandemic

IT WAS a warm spring morning in March 2020 when I woke up to the word in chaos. Outside, it all looked the same. The birds were signing, the sun was shining, and the routine activities of daily life were right there, waiting for me to take action. Little did I know that the moment I turned on the TV on that day, my normal, routine and peaceful world would change for long days, months, weeks, and even years to come.

The Coronavirus had arrived in Switzerland. Our sinister virus enemy from China had infiltrated our otherwise pure and fresh air from the Alps. The country's health authorities declared this invisible enemy a "pandemic," something so extremely dangerous and contagious that we had to stop all activity. Shops were closed. Public areas, restaurants, shopping venues, school, offices.

Wait a minute... I thought. Should we stop working and just sit and wait until the deadly virus is gone?

No way. We still had to work. Home offices became the new normal. Kids had to take their school classes online. Millions of families in the world had to stay home, stuck together in their little homes or apartments, with no possibility of going out. If you were a wealthy person and lucky enough to own your own house with a private garden and pool, then it probably didn't bother you much to stay at home. But, the reality in most countries was that the average family with two adults and two children lived in a much more limited space.

Those were certainly not easy times. At the time of writing (2022), when I look back, it even seemed like a dystopia. It was as if I had just awoken from a very bad dream. By the end of 2022, the Coronavirus had disappeared in Europe and there was another threat on the horizon, the so-called "Monkey Pox." This started gaining media attention right after the "Pride Month" of June, when millions of people from the gay and LGBT community and supporters dominated the streets to sing and dance to the song of love.

The Monkey Pox outbreak stole the attention from the media superstar that was COVID-19. However, the story never gained any traction despite the World Health Organization declaring it a global health concern and extremely dangerous. They had just hired the wrong PR specialists, I guess, so it vanished from the face of the Earth. Some scared people might have taken the vaccine.

But how did we get into such a mess? How could an apparently small respiratory virus cause a mass psychosis worldwide? There are, in my opinion, three main suspects: the media, the governments, and the industries who benefited playing with *fear* - our major weakness as a species.

If I turned the TV on to listen to the usual morning news in July 2021, all the channels were broadcasting the same thing: headlines remained focused on new COVID cases, and new variants coming in, despite high vaccination rates. It turns out, the danger was with the young people. Old people were not of concern anymore, as they were at the beginning of the pandemic back in spring 2020.

The reason, according to "science," was that the old people were not at risk anymore because, by that time, most should be vaccinated, at best, or at worst, dead. *The Independent* newspaper in England ran with the headline: "Exponential Rise in Covid cases in England driven by younger people."[1] (That's how they spelled it; the WHO preferred COVID.)

On another site you could read: "Covid doesn't discriminate by age"[2](npr.com).

Another headline from Spain: "Spain reports new rise in coronavirus infection rate as cases among young people continue to spike" (El País.com)[3].

Just out of curiosity, I checked another country, Brazil. A news headline read: "The Covid-19 cases in young people are steadily increasing, according to reports" (CNN Español)[4] (...which reports? They never mentioned).

Okay, last attempt to find another storyline. I checked the news from *The Economist* in Mexico. Let's see; first headline: "Increment in Covid-19 cases among young people, according to OPS"[5] (Pan-American Health Association). It was the same storyline, everywhere.

In the same article from the OPS, I read the following statement: "The hospitality rates among people below 39 years old have increased more than 70% in Chile, and in some areas of the United States, more 20-year-old people are being hospitalized due to Covid-19 than 70-year-old people".

If we rewind to spring of 2020, the headlines looked very different. Here is one from July 2020 in Australia: "Melbourne aged care is facing a coronavirus catastrophe..."[6] Premier Daniel Andrews alarmingly mentioned that "we will see more people die, particularly in aged care. The consequences could not be graver." The World Economic Forum, a leading voice in all economic matters surrounding the pandemic, showed a very interesting graph in early 2020 that showed "The fatality rate for people over 80 from COVID-19 is almost 15% according to data from

China" (...again, which data? The report fails to give those details).

So, in the data I read from the WEF website,[7] all people over 60 had a higher risk of getting the virus and dying from it in 2020. In July 2021, it was all about young people. How is it possible that the virus could "discriminate" younger people, who had apparently a nearly zero risk (with 0.2%) in 2020, and just the next year, suddenly revert the graph so that all the risk was with the young people? If "Covid doesn't discriminate by age," how did it manage to discriminate young people for an entire year?

The "best" part came toward the end of 2021. So, the Corona did not have enough with targeting the elderly, then the mature and young adults, going down to teenagers. Towards the end of 2021, kids below 12, small children and babies, also became a threat to society.

I still remember those radio advertisements in Swiss German (the native "slang" in the German part of Switzerland, where I live) that went more or less like this: "Hey, do you need more reasons to get vaccinated? What about this? "Sounds of friends gathering and laughing" ... or this? "The sound of the waves crashing, resembling holidays" ... or what about this? "The sound of music from a night club and people clinking glasses" ...

It was not about getting back our health anymore, but also, the vaccine would give us back our freedom; we would be able to travel, to meet our friends, and to even enter restaurants and bars, just by showing your Covid pass.

But wait a minute, toward the end of 2021, a more deadly, contagious, dangerous, and homicidal group became the target of all media, government and societal attack: the non-vaccinated, the renegades. Thanks to them, people were dying of Covid in the streets. Thanks to them, new variants had "emerged" out of their dirty bodies, full of bacteria and impurity.

Those people should be avoided at all costs, we were

told, and be prevented from joining society. Green Passes were created around the world, using a QR code, which had to be scanned at the entrance of any public facility, including hospitals, restaurants, public transport and cultural events. If your pass showed green, it was because you were either vaccinated or tested PCR negative.

If your pass showed red, you were to be dismissed from society. That, ladies and gentlemen, was not Orwellian 1984,[8] nor a fiction movie. This was the reality of 2021.

I admit, I belonged to this group of "terrorists." I could smell the trap. Having worked in biotechnology and pharma industries for a long part of my professional career, I was skeptical about the true existence and origins of the virus, the coordinated approach to tackle such a health crisis, and the time it took to develop and test the safety of the vaccines.

The amount of pressure exerted on the population worldwide to follow mandates that profoundly hurt our economies, families, and our health is not to be taken lightly. It is obvious that humanity needs constant interaction with others to survive. We need to breathe air properly, and it is unnatural to always be wearing something made with chemicals around your mouth and nose.

We need to meet with our families without fear. We didn't need to be forced to take a vaccine that was not even approved formally by the FDA when they did the rollout, jumping all security protocols and clinical trials needed to pass even the lowest of security measures.

Now, we cannot hide the elephant in the room. Was all this necessary? The destruction of our economies, the attack on our human affairs on the most basic level by locking us down, forcing us to give up our body sovereignty and to inject something that nobody had a clue what the effects would be... was all this worthwhile?

By now, we sadly have the answer. In the Summer of 2022, Europe experienced the highest death rate increase of

+16%, the highest increase on average in comparison to previous years between 2016-2021[9], the leading causes being reported as "unknown." Canada and the United States followed a similar pattern.

Thousands of doctors around the world have spoken up, exposing their findings about the corruption of the CDC (Center of Disease Control) in authorizing the release of those vaccines to the market without complying to even the lowest safety levels. Covid vaccines were never safe and effective.

Dr. Steve Kirsch, Dr. Robert Malone, Dr. Peter McCullough, Dr. Aseem Malhotra, Dr. Naomi Wolf, Dr. Joseph Mercola, just to mention a few, are publicly exposing the dangers of the vaccine, the enormous list of horrendous side effects, which include sudden death, cardiac arrests, encephalitis, myocarditis, blood cloths, and cancer, among others.[10]

There are thousands of studies proving the inefficacy, and even worse, the dangers of this vaccine. Dr. Steve Kirsch, in his article "Vaccine adverse reaction articles,"[11] compiled over 500 peer-reviewed articles documenting adverse reactions after the vaccines. He claimed there were over 1,250 articles in other peer-reviewed databases. Access to the database, REACT 19, can be found in the sources page at the references section.[12]

The vaccination mandates governments and unelected health authorities imposed on us in the name of the "common good," knowing the dangers of it beforehand, leaves us with the painful but obvious question: *Why?* Why would our own governments, doctors, and institutions together with the media, commit such a big crime against humanity?

What were their motivations?

I don't want to dig much further into trying to give an answer. That would need an entire book by itself, but many suspect it has to do with the Agenda 2030, which seems to be aimed at one global government, depopulation, and the trans-humanism agenda "in disguise."

Others believe it is just pure greed and hunger for power from big pharma and their acolytes working in the government and the public institutions, those same entities that are supposed to protect us from these very acts of corruption by establishing proper controls and protocols.

Some infamous names like Kill Bill (Bill Gates) or Klaus Schwab seem to be popular focuses of blame. Robert Kennedy Jr. published a very comprehensive book exposing the corrupted intervention of the NIAID (National Institute of Allergy and Infectious Diseases) under the leadership of Dr. Anthony Fauci, 'America's Favorite Doctor,' during the Coronavirus outbreak in America.

Kennedy's book, *The Real Anthony Fauci: Bill Gates, Big Pharma, and the Global War on Democracy and Public Health,* was a real eye opener for me, not only to understand the corruption on the highest levels of our "democratic institutions," but also to recall history and recognize previous patterns of pandemics which did not have the same success creating public fear, but were close enough.

By reading the book, I learned that the HIV-AIDS outbreak followed an almost identical media deployment as the COVID did in more recent times. Kennedy has investigated and written about this topic for many years, and through his Foundation Children's Health Defense, he has exposed the dangers of vaccination campaigns for children in general and how vaccines are linked to the current autism crisis in American children.

When the TV was off, and I stayed away from checking social media, reality looked actually quite different. I live in front of a beautiful forest. From my window, I could see the beautiful trees and deer. The deer seemed to be particularly cheerful, walking around, unimpressed by my presence. One day, I saw an elderly woman walking her dog. She was wearing a big blue face mask. At that moment, I could not help but feel a bit sorry for our human race. There was the deer, walking freely in the forest with no timetable to follow, and no need to wear a mask, with worry about any sickness.

The dog seemed quite relaxed, too, just sniffing at everything around. Why weren't dogs wearing a mask, by the way? They are as close to humans as they can be. Some dogs even sleep in the same bed as their owners.

From science, we know that all animals, plants, and other living organisms share the same DNA patterns as humans. We also know that we all share 99.9% of the same genetic structure,[13] and all living things are made of the same four basic elements: carbon, oxygen, nitrogen, and hydrogen.[14] So, why is it only us and not the rest of the living species that are affected by this virus? (Except, maybe for bats that are supposedly the "carriers" although no clear evidence proved that claim.)

So, here we are. Homo Sapiens, the "smartest species" on the planet. Wearing face masks in the open air. But it was not about science or health anymore, was it? It was about doing the "right thing." It was a fashion statement, the Status Quo. If you didn't wear a mask, you didn't belong. You "didn't care" about spreading your viruses to other people.

How dare you?

4. Naïve Childhood

FROM my most remote childhood memories, I still recall some distant sense of freedom. I remember I could run around, scream and play, with no sense of shame, and no worry about anything at all. I used to hang out a lot with my neighbors, two young boys around my age.

Every afternoon, we went on new adventures. One day, we would visit abandoned homes and imagine that we were ghost hunters trying to find hints about the ghosts' whereabouts. Another day, we would climb the park trees and eat apples from it. We would take our bicycles and explore the neighborhood, looking for new "territories" to conquer. I don't remember having any sense of time back then. It was all fun, and discovery, and freedom.

Those memorable afternoons kept diminishing the older I got and the more "responsibilities" I acquired from school. With more time spent at home, I also increased the amount of hours I watched TV. Coming from Mexico, and growing up in the 1990s, it was very common for a young girl like me to watch Telenovelas. I had my favorite ones: *Muchachitas*, *Alcanzar una Estrella*, and *Agujetas de color de rosa* are the ones I recall the most.

By watching Telenovelas, I started to get an idea about

what is supposed to be a good life growing older: meet a rich man, get married, and have kids. Basically, all the Telenovelas finished with the same happy ending: the rich and handsome man who met the poor young and beautiful lady, finally overcame all the obstacles and got married... happily ever after.

This seemed like a good plan. I spent my early teen years fantasizing about that; about finding my handsome prince that would marry me and have a family, and we would live happily ever after. However, the reality is that there is a very different world out there; one that I could not really grasp, because in my bubble of school and fantasy, that reality was out of my reach.

I recall just one memorable event where I could "see" what was going on in Mexico in the mid 1990s outside my pink world. I remember watching a national tragedy on TV in the spring of 1994. Luis Donaldo Colosio, the favorite presidential candidate from the right-wing political party Partido Revolucionario Insitucional (the infamous "PRI") had been shot dead during a campaign rally in the community of Lomas Taurinas, in Tijuana, Mexico.

That news shocked the entire nation. Many hours of narrative of the event followed during that tragic day. People were demanding to know who the killer was. Apparently, a young man shot him in the head for no apparent reason. Like in a good Hollywood movie story, they caught the "bad" guy within a few hours of the assassination and put him in prison. His name is Mario Aburto, and he was 23 years old at the time.

As a young girl, this story made a very big impression on me. I wanted to know more. I wanted to understand why someone would kill the famous, beloved, and popular presidential candidate that Colosio seemed to be. However, the stories on TV and the newspapers all followed the same story: He was shot by a young guy that had been sentenced to 48 years in prison. Case closed.

Life goes on.

Within days, a new candidate was named by the PRI. Life returned to normal for the majority of the people. I also eventually moved on. I had school to attend and my own life issues to worry about. It was time to immerse myself back in my pink bubble.

There were a few times when I did ask myself some questions.

For example, what would be the interest of that guy to kill a presidential candidate? Was it for money? Or for fame? I didn't think that somebody would be dumb enough to kill a famous personality during daylight and around thousands of people. However, my limited thinking capacity and my naivety at the time stopped me from questioning further. The bad guy was in prison. That should be enough.

After twenty-seven years, there was still a lot of mystery around the Colosio case. In recent years, Mario Aburto, the only apparent perpetrator of the assassination, asked to reopen his case in the Supreme Court. Although many journalists have attempted to find out the truth, Mario Aburto refuses to give many details about what really happened on the 23rd of March 1994. One journalist from *Los Angeles Times*, Jesús Lemus, once had the chance to ask him directly. In his report he relays the short conversation:[1]

"Did you kill Colosio?" Jesús asked.

"It is only propaganda. I did not kill him, but when can you win against the government? If they say you did it, you did it, and there is no way you can defend yourself against that; meanwhile, I am here, serving a sentence for something I did not do, spending my life incarcerated"- responded Mario Aburto.

. . .

It's a whispered secret. Everybody knows by now that the Deep Mexican State was involved in the assassination of Colosio. Hundreds of books and reports have exposed how Colosio was not following the "real" agenda of the political party he represented.[2] He became a threat to the Status Quo. That cost him his life. But, we, the Mexican population, what was in it for us? They gave us a Telenovela story, like we were used to. There was a good guy that got killed by the bad guy. The bad guy was found and put in prison. Now we could go on and live happily ever after.

You would be surprised how effectively this narrative works. People like to see good guys and bad guys. Life portrayed as a bi-dimensional phenomenon. Good and bad, tall and small, sick or healthy. The world seems more understandable when we measure it like this. There are victims and heroes, leaders and peasants, God and evil. Give us a good story with two sides and we follow. We believe. We want to believe that good people are in charge, and bad people are sent to prison. Don't we?

Reality finally hit me really hard one night in late March 1995 when my dad passed away. I was in sixth grade. Nobody from my family saw it coming. Just a night before, I'd had dinner with him. We discussed plans for the future, like which school I was going to join for secondary school. He helped me with my homework as usual, and then after dinner, we sat together around the sofa; he was reading the news, and I was hanging around with my little brother, listening to music.

The next day, he was dead. It was a car accident. He was 45 years old. Suddenly, my mom was left alone with three kids, at such a young age. To make things more complicated, my father had left a small business, with a big debt with the bank for land he had just purchased with two other partners. There was a house mortgage, and no life insurance. I was 11 years old. How was I supposed to take this? Why had nobody taught me at school or on TV what real pain feels like?

In school, I learned math, science, grammar and history. Nothing I had learned there prepared me for such a tsunami. Telenovelas were of no help either, obviously. There was no charming prince to look after me. No one could bring my father back. Welcome to real life.

I started to grasp that there are many realities out there. You can live in a bubble of illusions, which according to your own perceptions, all look very real. My pink world seemed very real. What I was learning at school felt very relevant, and important. But when the bubble broke, when I had to confront real pain, I started to feel like a puppet, being pushed around by random events and not really understanding my part in it. What was my role to play?

I wish someone would have taught me how to confront the harsh realities of life at an early age. Society somehow sees childhood as a place to construct and maintain a web of lies around life that does not really serve us when we grow older.

We are not taught to develop resilience, courage, and the ability to stand up and speak our minds. Rather, we learn to obey, to listen to the teacher for seemingly endless hours, to read only "official school textbooks" and nothing else, and to memorize useless data so we can pass the exams. Then, in my "free time" I was inundated by homework, doing more sums, multiplication tables, more basic geometrical shapes, and learning about "history" in the most basic way, memorizing dates of events and treaties.

What about the real-life topics? The economic crises, the corrupt governments, the increase in inequality, the pollution, the criminality, the addiction to substances like alcohol and drugs... all things that really affect society?

Those were left to "the adults" to deal with.

We kids did not need to worry. All we needed to do was

our homework, be good kids, eat all our dinner, and watch TV. One day, though, these kids will be the future of the nation. At eighteen, when they are "thrown into real life" after university, they find themselves, like I was, clueless about how the world really works, blinded by misinformation that leaves them directionless.

It can be too much stress to handle for a young adult that has "just come out of childhood." That's why, in our twenties, we tend to "rebel": party hard, get drunk, get high. Let's get numbed again, to extend a little the illusion of childhood where everything takes care of itself.

Perhaps this common pattern is another thing we need to adjust as we come to grips with our existing world of illusion.

5. The Illusion Of Having A Life On Social Media

IT WAS ALL FUN, when I joined Facebook in 2007. I was still in university, so it was a fascinating tool that allowed you to have all your friends on one network. There, we could post our party photos, exchange information on all sorts of events, and talk to each other. It was a great place to meet other people as well, and to learn (or nose around) the life of others.

I'm surprised how popular this way of socialization became after just a few years. Before, we only had mobile phones, emails, letters, landlines... and the most retro way... personal contact. If you were a guy in the 1980s and wanted a girl to be your girlfriend, you had to have the guts to go directly to her and tell her to her face.

Nowadays, that's what social media and dating apps are for. You can now choose the best possible picture to post about yourself and construct an attractive persona with the photos you upload and the catchy language you use. Is this real? As real as you want to believe it is. The advantage of social media is that you have an opportunity to build a completely remastered persona. Are you a bit overweight? Photoshop is the answer.

You don't have any relevant academic degree? No problem, make yourself an influencer or pretend to be an opin-ionated intellectual on X, formerly known as Twitter. You live in an ugly house or apartment? Fear not, you can use Instagram templates to embellish even the ugliest of places with flashy lights and neon colors. You have no friends? Nothing to worry about. Just pay for them! Facebook, Insta-gram, and X have specific services to make your page traffic increase.

You can change everything when building your online persona. In fact, I know friends who do it. I bet you have friends like that, too. Those who post their idyllic holidays, their endless social events, their latest outfit; the last visit to the gym, the green Thai chai latte from Starbucks that they just drank... their lives look perfect. And look at yours: you are overweight, have no money to go on holidays, no new outfit to show, and no exciting social life.

Why? Why is my life so miserable compared to others? Why can't I have the same, too?

Social media is the perfect environment to spread the deadly virus of victimhood. Because others have a better life, I should feel sorry for myself because I don't have it. And so, as an effort to not be "left behind" I produce my perfect life on the social media, too... but that doesn't help me, because I know it's all a lie. My life is really not better. If anything, I'm getting more anxious, and impatient. I'm losing the sense of reality where a persona has to work hard to get what they deserve. Seeing so many influencers and famous people in social media living the easy life makes you wonder what you can do to reach the same standard, without having to work your ass off. That is, if the pictures they present are reality.

So, where is this all heading? It seems we are going into a spiral with no end. The more we use social media, the more we tend to disassociate from our real life. In order to maintain our imaginary life, we need to spend an enormous amount of time backing it up with photos, comments, likes, and interaction with others. The more likes and attention you get, the more trapped you feel in the web. You feel that you "have to" keep posting, keep liking and commenting. The more you do it, the more the anxiety, and the impatience, and the feeling of loss you experience.

It's like aiming to reach the top of the mountain; the elixir of life, the ecstasy of fame and glory...and with every like or comment, you receive a little share of it, your dopamine levels increase... the excitement grows... but stays there just a microscopical amount of time. Your fame only lasts as long as the newsfeed allows, which is barely some seconds.

I found this out the hard way. I used to spend many hours of my day on social media, just to get a grasp of what it feels like to be "popular" and have someone pay attention to my life for once. But as a lifelong student of human nature, I knew that those spikes of satisfaction are very superficial and last only an instant. The truth is, people are more worried about themselves than they are about you. You cannot become popular or get attention unless you have paid attention to them first.

In the social media world, this means that if you want to get many followers and be popular, especially if you are not already a popular person or an authority of some sort, then you have to follow and comment on a lot of others first. If you like their pictures and feeds, they will correspond by liking yours. It's a mutual exchange of acceptance. On X, it is even a common strategy to gain followers: "#followforfollow means "follow me and I will follow back." Who cares who you are, and what your ideas about life are... I just care that you follow me and that's why I follow you.

It sounds pathetic, but that's pretty much how social media works. It's another world of illusions. The world online very rarely represents reality. But for some people, the online world has become more legitimate than the offline one. I am online, therefore I exist.

The addiction to social media and the amount of hours we spend in building a fake life, there sometimes seems to be a personal problem; but we are not alone in this. Actually, as Jaron Lanier[1] mentions in his book *Ten Arguments for Deleting your Social Media Accounts Right Now*, those tools have been specifically designed to create user-addiction.

Lanier quotes the former vice president of user growth at Facebook, Chamath Palihapitiya: "The short-term, dopamine-driven feedback loops we've created are destroying how society works...No civil discourse; no cooperation; misinformation, mistruth. And it's not an American problem, this is not about Russian ads. This is a global problem."

In the online world, all that matters is getting attention at all costs. That's why the social media platforms are built to show certain information in just a very short span of time. New information in the "newsfeeds" is flowing like a mad river at all times. If you want to catch up with what's going on with all your contacts, you must constantly keep scrolling back and forth...it seems like a pervasive present, never-ending, no limits attached.

This of course has consequences in the way we absorb and manage information. Short attention spans limit our capability to think deeply about any matter. Flash news and short comments replace long conversations and long research (reading books, looking around in the environment to get a better understanding) which leads to decreasing our ability to focus and work on a certain topic for long periods of time.

The question we need to ask ourselves here is the following: Why spend most of our time trying to feed our egos in the online world, where everything is just images and words, when there is a richer, more fulfilling and exciting world offline?

Humanity is always longing for connection. Therefore,

the promise of social media and the online world is very attractive and even addictive. The possibility of getting so much attention all day long triggers our dopamine levels in a constant manner. It is like getting your cocaine dose on a permanent basis. The more attention we get, the more addictive it becomes, and the more difficulty we have getting away from it and paying attention to the real world that happens outside the screens.

You may ask, as I did, what is the solution?

I propose we should act like wolves do when they want to achieve something unique: get away from the crowd. When you are a solitary wolf, you have to get in touch with a larger reality than the one normal members of the crowd see, and regard your perceptions as true. You find your own way to navigate through life circumstances. You develop a personality that allows you to solve problems based on information gathered through your own thinking and experience, rather than by following a pre-established collective thought process.

When you are in a social pack, the tendency is that you do things that please the crowd and become afraid to develop your own thinking. We become simply slaves of a broader system of moral beliefs that controls our own behaviors in favor of the "crowd."

I am not suggesting you become a complete anarchist and rebel against everybody and everything. But, when you make an effort to become more self-conscious of your thoughts, there is more chance of detecting which thoughts come originally from you, and which ones are influenced by external information like the media outlets and societal rules.

In Part 3 of this book, I will give you some practical tips on how to develop your own critical thinking, which will help you in your waking up process.

6. The Other Side Of Feminism

The dream of the perfect housewife

I CONFESS, I used to have a romantic idea about my role of being a woman. When I was a young girl, I loved to play with dolls. I dressed them, fed them, and made stories about their lives and whereabouts of their days. I took quite intuitively to my role as mother and main caregiver to my "sons and daughters." I must have been around five years old by then. At that time, I was not really conscious about the fact that as a girl, a female, I would play a specific role in society.

I remember copying what I saw around me: I learned that mothers carry their babies and take care of them; that they stay home and prepare the supper for the family; that a mother is someone that is always there, with a big smile, always willing and ready to attend the family.

I idealized the perfect life of a wife from the 1950s: The young lady that marries a young handsome man, they get married, buy a nice house with a big garden, and have children. The woman stays home, runs the household, and raises the children, while the man goes to work the whole day, only to come back at dinner time.

When the kids grow old, the stay-at-home mom gets some free time to spend on charities, social work, or passing her afternoons having coffee and going shopping with other fellow housewives. When the kids finally leave home and build their own families and the father retires, then the couple has free time to travel, and enjoy their autumn years.

Now I know that this romantic story was far from being the truth in most of the households at that time. One of the books that depicts a more accurate view of the lives of the housewives at the time is Betty Friedan's[1] *The Feminine Mystique*. She tells her own story: A housewife in the Post World War II era (end of the 50s, beginning of the 60s), in middle class America. In her book, she expresses the deep dissatisfaction that she, along with many other women in a similar situation, deeply felt about their life's fulfillment while focusing on housework, marriage, sexual passivity, and bearing children. As it turns out, most of those middle class, mainly white American women, felt dissatisfied in their role.

One of the most remarkable questions she poses the reader goes like this:

"Each suburban wife struggles with it alone. As she made the beds, shopped for groceries, matched slipcover material, ate peanut butter sandwiches with her children, chauffeured Cub Scouts and Brownies, lay beside her husband at night, she was afraid to ask even of herself the silent question-- 'Is this all?'" ~ Betty Friedan

This book, published in 1963, set the stage to redefine the meaning of feminism. It created a revolution, where women started to fight back for the right to choose a different destiny; the right to get a degree, pursue a career, become part of the economic force, and also have the

power to choose over her own willingness to have children. This was the preamble of the huge feminist movements that took place in the 70s and 80s, when much of what was claimed at the time from women like Ms. Friedan became a reality for millions of women in Western countries worldwide.

As it turns out, the pink story that most of the girls like me grew up believing in was painting a world that apparently did not match reality. No one in social circles, school, or even TV talked about the dissatisfaction involved in the housewife's role that, according to Friedan and attested by many others, had been permeating and affecting thousands of housewives worldwide.

What should we look for as women? What really makes us happy? Is it the freedom to choose? To have complete liberty about the decisions of what to do with our lives.

This is, apparently, what the feminist movements are standing for.

However, as with everything in life, those questions did not have a simple answer. One might think that reaching a certain level of freedom would ultimately lead to our complete happiness and self-realization.

Tucker Carlson,[2] in his book *Ship of Fools*, talks about how the role of being a woman is used as a tool for inciting political ideologies that do not really represent the best interest for the people. In a particular section where he discusses the effects feminism has had on the way that American society is being pictured today, he cited a very interesting finding.

The University of Chicago has been collecting data since 1972 for a project called "The General Social Survey".[3] The survey's purpose, according to their webpage, is to "Study the growing complexity of American society. It is the only full probability, personal interview survey designed to monitor changes in both social characteristics and attitudes currently being conducted in the United States."

The research, as Carlson indicates, found a surprising fact: Women have become dramatically less happy in the last forty years. The study indicated that in the first years of the study (in the 40s and early 50s), women reported greater happiness than men. However, over time, they progressively became less content.

This sheds light on the complexity of defining female happiness over just the definition of the roles in society. As we have seen in recent decades, thanks to feminist movements, the advancement of the role of women in society has been extraordinary. In most industrialized countries, the gender disparity in education and work opportunities for men and women have virtually disappeared.

In the United States, for the first time since the 80s, women are earning more college degrees than men, and the disparity is increasing. Single women in New York earn on average eight percent more than their male counterparts in a similar job. Women have more decision power over their bodies than ever before. They can choose it all: to become mothers, to pursue meaningful careers, to marry or stay single, to become a single mother... female freedom seems to be skyrocketing at exponential rates.

With all this in mind, the key question is: *Why aren't we getting happier?* If we now have plenty of freedom to choose what we want to do, earn more money and have more career perspectives than ever before, what is missing?

Does women's freedom have an expiration date?

I recall a video I saw some years ago on YouTube. The video was made by an Argentinian lady named Paula Schargorodsky. It starts with Paula attending the wedding of her last single friend. She was 35 at the time. Then, she explains how, in her early girl days, she followed the conventional path: went to school, studied, graduated from college, and found a job.

Then she explains how this perceived freedom keeps getting narrowed as one grows older. She says: "In your twenties, you are free to do whatever you want... have boyfriends, lovers, one-night stands, work, study... just like men. But female freedom has an expiration date. When you turn thirty, a conservative wall falls. At every social gathering, you are confronted with one silent question: When will you settle down?"

Paula's statement really resonated with me. When I saw the video, I was just turning thirty. I was doing very well economically: I had a good job, nice friends, and a stable boyfriend. I had enough financial freedom to do whatever I wanted: travel, party, live new and varied experiences, etc. However, the topic of marriage and having kids was something that never really left my mind. Having grown up in Mexico, I had a strong inclination to end up having a traditional life. The idea of getting married and start a family was the target ideal for my life.

In front of the place I was living with my boyfriend, there was a beautiful old villa that was converted into a kids' day care. I remember walking by on my way to work and observing the little kids running around and having fun in the garden. I truly enjoyed watching them and imagining that in some years, I would bring my own kids there.

Not so long later, it became a reality. But the point is that I intrinsically felt the need to be a mother. It didn't matter how well I was doing in my career. I had the right partner, and the natural next step for me was to get married and have children. The conservative wall that Paula refers to is quite real, in my experience.

When you are in your twenties, you think that you still have your whole life ahead of you, so you focus on trying to enjoy and get out of life as much as you can. I think this is how it should be in general. In your twenties, you are full of energy; you are at a crucial time of your life where you can go in any direction. I doesn't mean that you cannot completely change your life at a later stage, but it is true that what you do in your twenties will have a big repercussion in your later adult life and how it will unfold.

Women that married too early (i.e. in their early twenties) might have missed the opportunity to experience other things like having a greater degree of freedom while pursuing their study and careers. Some might regret it, while others do not really feel like they missed anything, because they didn't know anything else at the time.

When I talked to my mother-in-law, who has been a stay home mom her whole life, I asked her if she regrets taking the decision to be a stay home mom and would she have preferred to have a profession. Her answer shows humility and also a sense of reality: "I enjoyed staying at home, seeing my two boys grow. At that time, we didn't ask ourselves about any other possibility. Married women stayed home and that's okay. I know today is different."

Her answer was very interesting. It made me ask, why do we struggle with being a mother and/or having a career?

When I grew up, my own mother, who worked almost her whole life, always told me: "It is important that you study and get a degree, so you have something to defend yourself with, and you can work, in case something happens to your husband." I know she talks from experience, because exactly that happened to her, when my father died at the age of 45 and she was left alone with three small children. How can you argue that such advice is the wrong advice? I definitely took it as the best advice ever, and that's what I followed. I went on and studied an engineering degree, MBA, and did many specializations with the aim of becoming independent and having choices.

As women, it seems to me that we are always at that fine line between wanting to gain our freedom and our natural tendency to be nurtured and protected by a strong man. It is a scientific fact that confirms what we women already know by instinct. Women tend to feel more attracted to men that appear strong, assertive, and who are doing financially better than them. This seems true across species; male mallard ducks have bright and beautiful colors in their plumage, bright green and blue colors displayed in their head and necks. Bright plumage shows a female that this particular male is healthy and reproductive.[4] In that way, the majority of women prefer strong men to weak ones, as we follow the same natural mating mechanism of the animal kingdom.[5]

So, the question still remains: What really make us happy?

7. The Career Illusion

WHEN I THINK BACK to why I decided on studying and getting a degree, the prominent answer which I gave myself was the following: I want to have a career and excel in that career.

The mainstream activity we do nowadays, male or female, is joining the "race of life," the world of occupation, of careers and jobs, with the purpose of earning a living. Is it the only goal? Maybe looking back to the 50s, it was really the man's job to bring in money and put bread on the table. In modern times, however, people also relate their careers to something more transcendental. It is not only about the job, per se, it is also a way to find our life's expression. Through our work, we want to be seen, heard, and recognized, as valuable members of our society.

There are innumerable professions one can choose from. In industrialized countries, people tend to choose careers that support the development of technology and industry: management, business, economy, production, logistics, programming, robotics, marketing, sales, research, product-based science and so on.

In less industrialized countries, the main professions still focus on working with nature to grow what nurtures us and keeps us alive: food, water, shelter. There are other noble professions that are focused on the development of humanity: teaching, arts, philosophy, history, Earth-based science, and others. One can choose from countless possibilities to become a productive member of society. What catches my attention, however, is that nowhere do I see the role of being a mother as part of the list of potential "careers." Is becoming an investment banker more relevant nowadays than raising children?

When we say: "I want to be a mother and also have a career," are we discriminating and diminishing our primary duty in this life, which is the creation and growth of life?

It seems that it is not impressive anymore to be a mother. When I went to school, especially during my university years, I had no class or space where I could discuss with other girls how we saw our roles in society as professionals and potentially mothers. All the girls of my generation romanticized with the idea of becoming a businesswoman, landing a great job in a prestigious company, and at the same time, to finding a suitable partner, getting married, and starting a family. Yes, we wanted it all! But what is the price to pay? Nobody told me there was a (very expensive) price to pay.

Let's focus on the fact that most women today want to pursue a career. We see examples of successful career women everywhere: people around us, that boss that heads a division and has a family of three; that Hollywood artist that makes million-dollar contracts and also raises her kids. The model of being a woman participating in society portrays the successful businesswoman and mother. She can make it all happen! Get a great job, have a family, and excel at everything. Is that ever true?

Sometimes, I feel like that promise is a trap. Take a look at real world facts and ask yourself, how many working moms can really develop a thriving career without hurting the time spent with their family?

The real world tends to look quite different. When we join the workforce, we tend to end up having a job, but not a proper career. To really excel at a profession, whether it is as a business executive, a team leader, or another positions of power, you need to spend an enormous amount of time working. You have to work long hours. Work during weekends. Possibly travel.

Most women, especially with small children, would find it impossible to dedicate that much energy and time without having to leave their children practically under the constant care of someone else.

Women attracted by the prospect of a successful career tend to be perfectionist with themselves and those around them. So, it is not surprising that when they decide to start a family, they end up getting depressed, burning out, and developing mental disorders while trying to reach a goal mathematically impossible: Being 100% at work while being 100% a mother is impossible.

Repercussions in family and partnership

IN THE PURSUIT of having it all, we tend to ignore the byproducts derived from our decision to become "productive members of society." How does the family, as a nuclear institution of our societies, benefit from women pursuing a career at the expense of sacrificing time with their spouse and children?

Stevenson and Wolfers,[1] in their paper "The paradox of declining female happiness" found interesting discoveries about those implications. As the number of women joining the workforce increased, so did the legal and social institutions that granted more autonomous decision-making to individual and family matters, like the rights over marriage, children born out of wedlock, the use of birth control mechanisms, abortion, and divorce.

These changes in the social construct had profound

implications in family life. Stevenson and Wolfers found that divorce rates doubled between the mid 60s and mid 70s, but even if the divorce rate has been falling since the mid 70s, the amount of divorced people has continued to grow, and there was also a considerable increase in children born out of wedlock between the 60s and the 90s. It goes as far as concluding that "about half of the children in the US are not living with both biological parents."

This is indeed an alarming statistic. To threaten the family construct is to put in danger the foundation of our entire civilization. A functional family needs both parent roles so that the children can grow in a healthy, wholesome environment. Candace Owens, author of *Blackout: How Black America Can Make a Second Escape from the Democrat Plantation,*[2] mentioned that the nuclear family situation is even worse in black populations, where according to the Center for Disease Control and Prevention, nearly 70% of black children come into the world without a father in the household.

By taking away the moral obligation of men to sustain a child, and at the same time pushing women to take more government support and money to back them up financially, seems not to be the solution to finding a happily ever after life.

8. Going Back To Basics

YOU MIGHT CALL ME a conservative, but after all these years living through all the "hype" of studying and preparing myself to become a professional woman, I still believe that, after everything is said and done, the most important role that I have as a woman is to take care of the preservation of our species by having children and building a loving family.

I am sure that many women might disagree and find the freedom to choose what to do with their lives the most important thing. Not all women wish to have children and form a family. Others prefer to focus on their jobs, to travel around and live many other adventures.

In my personal experience, I suspect that the idea to study and build a career did not really come from my internal desire as a child, but more from society's expectations. After all, I loved to play with babies and build family houses when I was young.

This conviction grew stronger in me when I heard a podcast by the renowned psychologist Jordan Peterson[1] where he gets questioned on what he thinks about the dramatic decrease of births and the fact that more than 50%

of women today are childless by the age of 30, something that is unprecedented in our entire history as a civilization.

To my surprise, his response was: "We (society) lied to them all the time." The first lie that gets implanted on us at a very early age is that we live in a patriarchy, a male-dominated world that is oppressive and does not leave enough space for women to have careers. The second lie is the belief that the most important thing in our lives as a woman is to have a career. The third lie is the belief that there is nothing that makes a woman more successful and gains them more prestige than their careers.

I believed all those lies and worked my way through the checklist. And as predicted, by the age of 30, my own conservative wall fell, and I realized that I wanted to become a mother and have a family. That is precisely what I did. I do not regret it for a single moment. Even though I enjoy working and having a profession, it is definitely incomparable to the joy of being a mother and raising children. The jobs I had in the corporate world when I was single felt so insignificant and inconsequential compared to the biggest task of taking care of your small child, that divine gift from God.

To close this chapter, I would like to reflect on the opening question: *As a woman, can we have it all?* My answer would be no, and we shouldn't even try if we want to keep some mental sanity. The fantasy idea of having a top career, becoming the top of your profession and being a wonderful mother is simply unrealistic and incompatible with real life. This is indeed, another dissolved illusion.

Part Two

Stay Away From Toxic Ideologies

MOST PEOPLE believe that they live in the truth. After all, our daily lives are a proof of what is real: the house you live in, the family you have, the work you do. We also think that our thoughts are part of that truth. After all, my thoughts represent me, right? It is even written in most constitutions of democratic societies: the right to think and express freely.

The vast majority of people remain unaware of the immense amount of manipulation we are exposed to from the day we are born. When we are young, we basically follow what our parents and teachers tell us without much questioning. We watch TV and movies and form a view of the world based on all that exposure. I think, sadly, humans lead just a very tiny fraction of their lives truly free, and that might be limited to the time from when we are born until the moment we have to attend school. For me, that was around four or five years old. I have also seen this transition with my two children.

I have experienced, as a mother, how they express themselves and say what they really want, even if what they wanted doesn't match what I wanted for them. My toddler, for example, loved his red sandals. He wanted to wear them everywhere, no matter what. When it was raining, I wanted to force him to wear the rain boots, but my little one refused vehemently. I eventually left behind the frustration of trying to make him wear what I wanted or thought was more appropriate for him and went with his choice.

I didn't need to understand his reasons. He simply wanted to wear them, and he fought for his wish, even if it was raining outside. I let him take his sandals and he happily went to play outside. He got his little feet wet, but at the end of the day, it didn't matter. He loved to get his feet wet and he had so much fun. I learned my lesson.

Over the years, though, with so much influence coming at us from all directions, we start to mold ourselves to "fit" in society. We give up our own desires in favor of following more generic trends. We trade our uniqueness in exchange for belonging to a group by doing similar things, liking similar things, and acting similarly.

Humans are, by nature, social creatures, so the need to belong dominates most of our existence. Unfortunately, this need to belong has been weaponized to implant ideologies that do not necessarily help us become better humans. On the contrary, those ideologies used to accumulate power and influence come from the intentional desire to keep us divided and in a constant fight with one another.

This is what I call toxic ideologies. If you take a look at the world today, and you try to look at it from some distance, you will realize that our societies are organized by ideologies. Ideologies are nothing more than a group of ideas and beliefs through which we try to explain the world. They are the basis for the creation of laws, policies, religions, and other institutions. You can develop your own ideology, but in most cases, we tend to follow an ideology that belongs to a group that we resonate with.

Religion is an ideology. Policies are ideologies.

Economic principles are ideologies. Even science is rooted in an ideology: the belief that we can observe and question natural events and attempt to give an answer through predefined scientific ideals. Basically, everything we believe comes from the primary act of having an idea.

We need to become aware that when we engage in ideologies, instead of uniting us in love, they increase the gap of disunion, distrust, and separation. The biggest desire of humans is connection. Ideologies, when rooted in love and unity, help the purpose and bring us forward.

The problem is that in the name of other greedy interests, some people who are hungry for power and influence use that need of human connection to manipulate others in ways that result in a bigger profit for the manipulator, but at the end, brings us to more disconnection and disunion. They implant toxic ideologies, sometimes so subtly that most people have no idea they are being manipulated into falling prey to their destructive influence.

At this point, you might be asking, how can we know which ideologies are rooted in love and unity and which ones are rooted in disconnection and fear?

Let's explore some of the current ideologies dominating society today, especially in Western areas, and which are causing a profound effect in people.

9. Toxic Ideology 1: White Supremacism

T HE TITLE of the ideology itself evokes nothing but a strong sense of disunity. Most people have strong opinions about it. I have difficulty even trying to make sense of this ideology in a way that brings me something positive.

According to the dictionary, white supremacy is a set of "beliefs and ideas purporting natural superiority of the lighter-skinned, called white human races, over the rest of the other racial groups." It is deeply rooted in history. But not only that, also deeply rooted in all our human affairs, independently of the country you live in.

When I was at school, I learned about colonization, and it went more or less like this: Mexico was once a country rich in racial diversity. We had more than 80 ethnicities,[1] which are called "indigenous" today. Then the white-skinned Spaniards came, trying to impose their superiority through religion and their ways of living when they saw all the vast resources that the land and its people had to offer.

They would conquer Mexico and establish the Catholic Church and la Nuova Spania because they had "superior" arms and better fighting tactics. Not even the Aztecs, one of the most advanced and powerful civilizations in Mexico, could defeat the Spanish army.

From there comes the term "Indio" for a native Mexican, coming from the word indigenous, which actually meant "coming from India." Mexican society has historically used Indio as a racist slur for indigenous people, who are mainly darker-skinned, and form part of the "poorer classes" on the societal hierarchies in Mexico. When I investigated the source of the word "Indio" it came to me from many sources that it was actually a mistake of Cristobal Colón (Christopher Columbus), who believed that he had arrived in India and started to call everybody "Indios."

It is interesting that the word prevailed overtime and that the connotation was used in a negative way, even though the meaning of the word itself has nothing to do with any racial discrimination.

This is one of many other examples that portray the colonization of "colored humans" by "white humans" over the centuries.

Other infamous examples include the apartheid era in South Africa, the British colonization of India, the dark times of slavery in America, and of course, one of the most sinister of all, the Nazi era. All those historical events have as a root one single problem: white supremacist practices. Nobody can deny that any form of racism is atrocious. But those stories reinforce a belief that white people are the oppressors and peoples of "color" are the victims.

How exactly did that ever happen? Were the motives purely racist, or is there something else behind it? When exactly did all these races in the world simply let themselves be subjected to "white powers"?

I can hardly believe that all those horrible events were caused for a single reason. I've never understood why such wars had to exist in the first place. When I try to look for an explanation, the typical answer I get is: "White people live in the north and darker people in the south. Because the south is a more fertile environment and the sun shines longer, there is more abundance of rich foods and minerals. That's why white people come to the south and try to dominate with violence so that they can get all the resources and make darker people their servants."

That's basically the only version we get from our school textbooks and history channels and is seen as a mainstream accepted truth. But something in this story, as logical as it may sound, still does not convince me that it is the truth. How, why, and when was it decided that white people should govern over other races?

The Caucasian race founded Western society and have become the dominant race in Western civilization. And as we know today, Western values are being systematically destroyed. Let's not forget that Western civilization, despite its many faults, is still one of the freest societies in the world. It is where we see some sort of democracy, although not perfect. This is the only civilization today where you can build a strong middle class with good living standards. And yes, it happens that the dominant race in the West is white.

Why is that so wrong?

The targeting of whites, males, and Christianity

IN 2017, there was a strange gathering called the "March for Science," a global event where thousands of people marched in favor of science and the role it plays in everyone's lives. This was organized as a response to Donald Trump's supposed "anti-science and anti-climate agenda."

Canadian professor Gad Saad[2] investigated the mission statement of the march founders and found this on their website: "At the march for science, we are committed to centralizing, highlighting, standing in solidarity with, and acting as accomplices with Black, Latinx, Asian and Pacific islander, Indigenous, non-Christian, women, people with disabilities, poor, gay, lesbian, bisexual, queer, trans, binary, a-gender and intersex scientists and science advocates (...)"

Ahem. By this logic, if you happen to be white, male, heterosexual and Christian, sorry my friend, your work cannot be supported. Does that sound like real science?

The funniest part comes when clearly privileged white people like the American President Joe Biden mention proudly that white supremacists are the biggest threat to the United States. Being white and privileged, I do not see why he has anything to complain about. According to the world of political correctness: Male + white + heterosexual = Toxic masculinity.

I do not by any means support violence against anyone just because of the color of their skin. Events like the apartheid or the Nazi era were terrible and should have never happened. Nothing justifies the violence. Why do we keep the wound open?

Why did major media channels like MSNBC have dedicated programs hosted by black people with the single purpose of criticizing white people? Yes, you read that right. Just listen to any podcast from Joy Reid as an example. When I found out about this, I was shocked. This was 2022, using the ancient tactic of hate speech against races to keep us divided.

It has not always been the white males who are the "bad guys" of the story. Just twenty years ago, the "bad race" was actually the Middle Eastern, olive-skinned, young guys who were judged as "potential terrorists" and "Islamic extremists" and who hated America and the West.

Wars on race are one of the most effective weapons used by governments to keep the masses distracted and fighting over something that is mainly an ideology. *Divide et Impera* (divide and rule). It has worked for centuries. It worked for the United States as a justification to go to war with the Middle East on multiple occasions, for reasons that we will never know if true or not. Just to give an example, take the September 11th event. The story they wanted us to believe is that the destruction of the Twin Towers in New York City was committed by some random Islamic terrorists who hated America and were in close contact with Osama bin Laden, the Supreme Leader and head of the entire operation.

Imagine the level of intelligence that is accredited to Osama bin Laden, to outsmart the entire the FBI, CIA, the entire American Defense Department, the Federal Aviation Administration (FAA), the North American Aerospace Command Program (NORAD), the U.S. Military, and all sorts of organizations involved with keeping American territory secure.

Four random terrorists nobody knew about and with no criminal records could suddenly master commercial aircraft in such a way that not only could they hijack them, take them off of any radar, crash into and cause the collapse of monumental towers more than 400 meters high, weighing 250,000 tons and made mainly of steel and concrete?[3] The other plane would crash into the Pentagon, the official building of the U.S. Department of Defense? How hilarious.

I don't want to get into the details of this story, which everybody already knows, but if you are interested in reading an extremely well documented book about September 11 and what really happened, I recommend you get the book *The Trigger* by David Icke.[4]

My point here is not to discuss whether the explanation for what exactly happened on September 11 was true or not. The point is that this event triggered a long-scale and devastating war in the Middle East based mainly on ideology and race. Now, 23 years later as I write this, the Islam extremists are not the biggest threat to humanity.

Now the white supremacists, the founders of the West, the civilization that went to war with the Middle East just a few decades ago for representing a "Threat to the West" are now the threat. And what are the values the West stands for? It might not be the perfect societal construct, but if people, and especially the government, would stand for the true values of freedom, justice, democracy, the right for individualism, patriotism, free enterprise and personal responsibility, we would be living in another world today.

10. Toxic Ideology 2: Gender Equality And Transgender Movements

I'M HONESTLY NOT SURE what gender equality means anymore. In the good old days of common sense and scientific reason, we had just two genders: Male and Female, so just she/her, he/him. Gender equality meant having equal rights for men and women.

In today's world, this is outrageous and discriminating. You are not including the gender-fluid, queer, non-binary, trans... human beings who have the right to self-identify as something other than being a "man" or a "woman." (Are there other living entities included?). If you want to make sure you are being inclusive to everybody, you have to use neutral pronouns. I came across a list of 78 pronouns you can use.[1]

Those are:

He/She -- Zie, Sie, Ey, Ve, Tey, E
Him/Her -- Zim, Sie, Em, Ver, Ter, Em
His/Her -- Zir, Hir, Eir, Vis, Tem, Eir
His/Hers -- Zis, Hirs, Eirs, Vers, Ters, Eirs

Himself/Herself -- Zieself, Hirself, Eirself, Verself, Terself, Emself

So, now if you want to write an email to someone you don't know, maybe it is wise to ask them which pronoun they feel identified with, otherwise you will hurt his/her/hirs/eir/em/x/z/y feelings.

Don't ask me when to use which pronouns. I have no clue. Maybe you can freely choose? Maybe if I suggest one or two, I'm being already a criminal discriminator?

If you want to be on the safe side, just identify yourself with your pronouns to encourage the other person/being to share theirs. Do not force them, because it may hurt the feelings of the person... and be careful, because you could even get sued.

It happened to Professor Nicholas Meriwether, a professor of Political Philosophy at the Shawnee State University in Portsmouth, Ohio. During his class, a student raised his/her/its... hand to make a comment about the class, and the professor replied with "Yes, sir." The student felt offended, because they identified as a woman, but the professor refused to call them a "her," replying that his Christian values stopped him from recognizing a gender in a person which he believes is false, but he agreed to call the person by their last name.[2]

Long story short, there is no clear settlement between the parties up to now. What I felt curious about the situation is the reaction of the school officials. They argued that Professor Meriwether created a hostile environment by refusing to respect the person's preferred pronoun. And for this reason, he could be fired or suspended without pay, for violating nondiscrimination policies. I wonder: Why is it just discriminatory to refuse to accept someone else's ideology of gender, but it is completely okay to violate Christian values? Where is the logic here?

In late March 2023, there was news about a mass shooting[3] happening in a Christian School in Nashville, in the United States. Six people were killed, including three nine-year-old kids. The shooter was a 28 year-old transgender, self-identified as "she" although recently changed to "he." The mainstream news did not want to reveal the "motives" behind the shooting, although it is known that the police found many documents written about the reasons and even a plan of the building among the shooter's belongings.

The slant in the news seemed to be about the fact that guns are still allowed to be owned by individuals in America, and that is what needed to be addressed.

Why do I make reference to this? Because in the whole tragedy, the media seemed to ignore the fact that the aggressor was a transgender, an anti-thesis of Christianity. Why was the news ignoring that the main issue behind this was not the use of guns, but the apparent hate against Christians from transgender communities?

Christian values are indeed the antithesis of transgenderism. Christians believe that you cannot violate God's laws, and you should accept that you do not have God's powers to change your biological sex. Transgenders believe the complete opposite: they can change their sex at any moment, just by believing in the idea and changing their pronouns.

So here you see two apparently unrelated news events. In the first one, a professor is suspended from his profession for defending his Christian beliefs. In the second event, the transgender person that commited the crime of murder against Christians barely got mentioned, and in fact, the political tone of the news was that we should "regulate gun ownership."

This is indeed a twisted world. If a man identifies as a

woman, to me, this seems more like a mental problem rather than a biological problem. Our sex is embedded in our genes, in every fiber of our cells, in the very source of our creation. The belief that a baby can be confused about his or her identity is to arrogantly say that the evolution of humankind simply got it wrong. Dr. Hawkins argues in his book *The Power vs. Force* that the basic law of the universe is the law of economy. That means that the universe does not waste a single speck of sand. Every single cell, every single thing that exists in the universe serves a specific purpose and is meant to fit into a perfect equilibrium. There is no such thing as "mistakes in nature."

I don't want to talk about worse scenarios: people identifying themselves as unicorns, horses, dogs, cats, bigenders and genderfluids. There is simply no space for arguments. By the way, do you know that the gender unicorn exists? I will leave for you to read about what it entails to identify as a unicorn in the sources[4] at the end of the book, from educational material targeted at kids or young people, provided by the state of California.

The gender equality movement has been changing its victims over time. It went from gaining equal rights for women in the workplace back in the late 60s, all the way to being 'inclusive' with men identifying as women and women as men, and men with unicorns and unicorns with horses and... it simply includes everything.

In my opinion, this is a very toxic ideology. It keeps us away from our truth, from the source of our origins and from who we really are. God created us perfectly. We are part of his perfect and wonderful creation, divine and wonderful beyond words. Each man and woman has their own roles in life which are crucial to keep our societies thriving and alive.

Men cannot get pregnant, women can. Men have strength, endurance, assertiveness; qualities that were developed in ancestral times to keep their families safe from danger. Women have compassion, care, delicacy and empathy, qualities that help in raising children and keeping family union.

Denying our very nature may look like a trendy thing today, but it will have catastrophic consequences for humanity if we don't connect back to reality. When we are disconnected from what is real, we become prone to endless manipulation. We become malleable and fall prey to whoever makes us feel that we "belong," even if that means losing ourselves.

Gender equality is a toxic destructive ideology for three reasons:

1. It denies your nature.
2. It keeps you in constant anxiety and with a sense of disconnect, making you more aggressive.
3. It incites you to deliberately hate your natural body by constantly wishing to be someone else.

Every time I read in the news that somebody has changed their sex to be able to 'finally be happy' or 'feel comfortable in their own skin' I can predict the road to depression or even suicide.

A man that cuts his penis off to get a vagina will never experience an orgasm like a woman does. Same case with women getting a penis. As much as technology has advanced to make a woman look like a man and man like a woman, we can never play God. To believe politicians, scientists, feminists, and all those people supporting such movements, is to condemn ourselves to our own destruction. A confusion in gender creates insecurity, deep anxiety, depression, sadness, confusion, and disconnection.

A person feeling true in himself or herself, completely

accepting their body, their gender, their soul, is a person that will feel more connected to life and will live a happier life.

Now, here is a disclaimer. I am not against gay people, or lesbians. I respect their choice, and it is not my business to judge whether they are happy or not. I have friends who have chosen that path, and I love them and respect them dearly. There is a big difference between consciously acknowledging your sexual preference without denying your gender nature and being a self-identified woman who can have children despite having male sexual organs and who attacks anyone delimiting the meaning of a woman. The latter sounds definitely scary.

To believe in such toxic ideologies is to deliberately be ignorant of our origins. To delete everything that has existed, all the millions of years of evolution that converted us from chimpanzees eating fruits in the tropical forest to hunter-gatherers, all the way to the sophisticated beings that we are today. How can we destroy eons of divine intelligence in just ten years and simply believe in rainbows and unicorns?

The Bible has a wonderful message in Mathew 10:39 that says: "Self-sacrifice is the way, my way, to finding yourself, your true self. What kind of deal is it to get everything you want but lose yourself? What could you ever trade your soul for?"

What is the point of denying the truth of your identity? There is just one answer: Self-hate. This ideology has nothing to do with inclusion or unity and everything to do with losing yourself and losing contact with the real-life forces that live within you, which is your own truth.

I don't ask you to believe me or to agree with my philosophy, but please give it a thought. In a world of mirrors and lies, we often find that nothing is what it appears to be.

11. Toxic Ideology 3: Political Correctness

WHILE TAKING A BREAK from writing, I came across a very interesting documentary produced by the Spanish biologist and professor Fernando Lopez-Mirones[1] called "The Selfish Monkey." It made an impression on me because it tells the story of our evolution in a fascinating way. We came from being small, monkey-like creatures admiring the big kings of the jungle, like elephants, lions, and bears... to basically ruling over them.

We have the extraordinary ability to become self-conscious and also conscious of our environment. We gained mastery over the elements. Little by little, we started to build our own jungle, huge concrete caves where we could stick together. We now call them megacities.

In these megacities, we could not behave like we did in ancestral times when we stayed in small crowds. In those small crowds, it was very clear who the alpha males were, who were the leaders, and which ones the caregivers. In megacities, where so many people are stuck together in smaller spaces, it becomes very difficult to display your "superiority." It can be simply too dangerous to do so.

Humans are territorial. We are not used to being in huge crowds in limited spaces, like ants or bees. It is not our true nature. We like to conquer and expand territories. We like our own space. And we are selfish. That's why we needed a mechanism to be able to co-exist and protect us from killing each other. With the birth of civilization came the concept of political correctness.

Civilizations are a complex setup of human interaction which have certain characteristics[2] like shared language, shared religion, culture and tradition. In that sense, political correctness could be seen as a set of rules in communication that help people stay away from conflict by avoiding offensive language.

So, where do we draw the line between being free to express your thoughts and keeping civilized language to avoid conflict?

Suppression of speech has been an eternal battle. I think it is as ancient as the ideology of Hell and Heaven. Over centuries, civilizations, and especially the politicians, religion, and people of law have demonized people that dissented from the "mainstream truths" of the era. Socrates, Aristotle, Copernicus, Gandhi, among many others rebellious geniuses, were killed or threatened with death for spreading their innovative ideas to the public.

In the 21st century, political correctness is taking on a different dimension. With the advance of technology, even regular people can suffer from speech suppression if they "misbehave" on social media. You don't have to be a rebellious genius fighting against the mainstream narrative presented to us by sponsored media. All you need to do to be silenced and censored, and judged about your thoughts, is to write something, record something, or say something that questions whatever mainstream truth of the moment in any of the mainstream social media.

Political correctness is becoming a dangerous tool for the suppression of free speech for the masses. There is a difference between trying to communicate in a peaceful, but truthful manner, and suppressing opinion because someone else may consider it offensive, racist, aggressive, etc.

But where is the line? How can I know if I am crossing the line between being truthful with my communication and being politically incorrect?

After the American election in November 2024 when Donald Trump won a second term as President, many people on X, particularly anti-Trump celebrities, announced they were leaving X for another social medium called Bluesky. Elon Musk, owner of X, touted his platform as upholding free speech, but the departees felt oppressed. To each his or her own. This kind of argument goes on a lot on so-called "social" media.

My common sense tells me that you cannot simply classify every single "offense" as "hate speech." In a free and mature society, people should be able to say what they feel, regardless of what others think. If someone offends you, you simply have to grow some balls and decide what to do with that offense. Do you accept it? Ignore it? You can choose. That is in your power. What is not in your power is to take away the right of the other person to express their opinion.

That's where I see a dangerous shift in current world events.

The COVID pandemic is a classic example. In 2020 and 2021, to be skeptical about the virus and the whole narrative, as ridiculous as it was. (I mean, who really believes that the virus came from a bat in a filthy remote Chinese market and then travelled to Italy on an airplane, where the first Western COVID case was found?) If you disbelieved the mainstream story about the origin of the virus, however, it meant you were a conspiracy theorist, a denier, and ignorant.

The "science" that failed to follow its own Hippocratic standards and the Koch laws to determine the existence of any virus, was telling normal people who thought critically that they were "dangerous" to society by not getting a vaccine. A vaccine that we know now (November 2024) did not work, because people still got COVID, and neither did it help avoid being transmitted because fully vaccinated people were still passing it on to others. In retrospect, the vaccine and its subsequent "boosters" simply failed to keep people safe and healthy.

Let's take a look at some numbers. In Switzerland. Swissmedic, which is the country's health regulator authority, reported the following data: as of 26 of August 2022, more than 15,000 reports of adverse effects related to the COVID vaccine were registered. Out of those, around 9,000 were not serious and 6,000 serious[3]. Switzerland has a population of 8 million people. From those, around 6 million had at least one dose.

It is well known that 90% of the people do not report adverse events to the health regulators. The majority do not even associate a sickness coming from a specific treatment. Taking all this into account, it looks rather alarming to me that out of the 15,000 reports that were received, 6,000 of them were serious adverse effects. I mean, that's 40% of the cases! And serious effects are cardiac disorders, nervous system disorders, musculoskeletal and connective tissue disorders, gastrointestinal disorders, skin disorders... that is alarming enough to remove the questionable vaccines from the market. Why did nobody say anything about these facts in the mainstream media?

Even now, if you dare to say something about it in some social circles, you are still considered a conspiracy theorist and ignorant. How would a nobody like you question the Bill Gates and Dr. Faucis of the world? For too long, the so-called "unvaxed" were not even allowed to enter public spaces, because they were considered dangerous and immoral. This is political correctness in its most sinister disguise.

The same is true with the climate change trap that I will explain in the next sections. I can offer many examples of how "political correctness" is being used as an instrument to suppress not only free speech, but our liberty as a whole. It is a very dangerous game, and we can end up being the boiling frog of lore. We do not see the imminent danger right away because it arrives gradually, little by little. If such social measures continue as I've discussed here, one day we will be cooked to death. Unless we jump!

12. Toxic Ideology 4: Climate Change And Over-Population

T HE WORLD has been in immediate peril for as long as I can remember. Year after year, we are reminded that there is not much time left until an apocalyptic climate event will finally erase us from the face of the Earth.

I still remember Al Gore's speech saying the ice poles would melted by 2013. And the many countdowns about how much longer we will stay around until we literally fry.

It turns out that the enemy of the world is carbon dioxide emissions, or so the story goes. This dangerous gas emission is a by-product of a civilization that uses too much fossil fuel. The mainstream story often forgets that carbon dioxide has a fertilization effect and is the main chemical responsible for photosynthesis, the living mechanism of plants, and that the more carbon dioxide that is emitted, the bigger the plants will grow, and the more life will flourish.

Are we still so naïve to believe that carbon dioxide emissions are the biggest enemy of humanity and the environment? Will neutralizing carbon save us from burning in Hell? Will "morally green" choices like replacing fossil-fueled cars with electric ones, stopping eating meat, stopping all plane travel, recycling plastics and PETs, and investing in solar panels have the desired effect of actually reducing temperatures, or are these well-intentioned but ignorant and completely useless choices?

According to global climate experts like Bjorn Lomborg,[1] we can't really fix climate change. Even if all the nations of the world complied 100% with the Paris Accords goal of limiting global warming to well below 2 degrees, preferably to 1.5 degrees Celsius in 100 years, spending trillions and trillions of dollars along the way, the reality is that as technology and industries keep evolving along with our civilization's needs, the carbon intensity will keep rising, and we will use more and more energy than ever before, which makes this goal completely unattainable.

There is no single nation in the world today that can rely fully on solar or wind energy to cover all their energy needs. Governments spend more than 40 billion USD every year subsidizing inefficient solar energy and wind power. With our current technology, the WEF (World Economic Forum) brags that we reached the 10% mark of use of solar and wind energy worldwide in 2021. Even if that were true, how are we planning to achieve the remaining 90%?

Carbon dioxide emissions are of course a by-product of "cheap" energy delivered by fossil fuel, which took us two hundred years of development. To think that we can replace fossil fuels and become "carbon neutral" worldwide by 2030 is a fairy tale dream that will cost trillions of dollars. And countries bragging about such ambitions do not include China, which is one of the top fossil fuel consumers worldwide.

Maybe in countries like the USA, Germany, or Switzerland this is plausible. But what about the world's poorest nations that don't have trillions to spend? Poor countries, especially in marginalized areas, desperately need cheap power and energy to sustain their societies and economies. Energy is the main source of growth and life, as it is for all nations still today. No single nation can realistically survive on solar and wind alone. At least, the technology is not there yet. So why make a big drama about it?

In 2023, Germany closed its three remaining nuclear plants – Emsland, Isar 2, and Neckarwestheim. In retrospect, this was regrettable with regard to supplying power during the German winter, because on 26 September 2022, the Nord Stream 1 and Nord Stream 2 natural gas pipelines, two of 23 gas pipelines between Europe and Russia, were rendered inoperable by a series of underwater explosions and consequent gas leaks occurred on 3 of 4 pipes. Keeping Germany warm in the winters of 2022 and 2023 was a difficult prospect.

Why are governments supporting leftist agendas that radicalize the ideologies around climate change to pass laws that make the poor poorer and the elites richer? Why do they not think of contingencies for the future when it comes to providing adequate energy for its citizens?

We might find part of the answer if we take a look at worldwide protests happening everywhere, and which are hidden by the mainstream media outlets. Mainstream media never shows that more than 30,000 farmers from the Netherlands threaten to stop the nation's food supply in protest of the extreme "climate policies" to eradicate "pollutant gases" by 2030. Using common sense, even if Dutch farmers cut more than 70% of their gas emissions, the Dutch plans will not reach the goal and will possibly destroy a vital part not only of the Dutch food supply, but also on a worldwide level in the process.

Let us not forget that the Netherlands is the second largest exporter of agricultural commodities in the world, just behind the USA.[2]

Similar protests happened in France when farmers protest government policies. A procession of tractors drove into Paris and some farmers sprayed manure and rotting produce on government buildings.

Another case was the mass protests in Germany over

excessively elevated gas prices and the shut-down of the afore-mentioned nuclear energy plants.

It's only logical. If natural gas is unavailable in winter, are the Germans expected to survive the harsh weather based on solar panels alone? This is when the sun "shines" there basically four hours a day?

In the United States, President Joe Biden announced a plan to call for a "climate change national emergency" which would allow him to take drastic measures against fossil fuels.

All of these events happened while heads of state and English Prince Harry were flying on private jets all around the world to chastise citizens for "abusive consumption."

All I see when looking at climate emergency speeches and faulty energy policies by governments everywhere is pure and sheer hypocrisy of politicians hungering for power.

I agree that we can do much better at managing our waste and finding ways to reduce the pollution we produce as a species. However, we can do little if we do not deal with the true sources of the problem. The real pollutants are the same people preaching they know better by restricting us and cutting away the energy and essential resources that we so much need to keep striving as a civilization.

Those politicians and industry cartels are the ones who generate the problems that they claim they are trying to solve. Or, let's ask Coca-Cola how they stole precious pure and drinkable water from marginalized communities in Mexico so that they could use that water to produce more Coke (while polluting Mexico's underground water sources, producing more plastic, and emitting enormous pollutants during the manufacturing and distribution process). Those communities might not have drinkable water for domestic use, but take a look at their small corner stores, and you will find full stacks of Coca-Cola bottles!

Let's keep our eyes wide open and stop believing in climate change propaganda. Let's observe who really benefits from this and who the real losers are.

Let's face some inconvenient truths:

1. We cannot change the climate with our small daily actions (but geoengineering on the military level can change it on the surface).
2. Nothing we do will have any noticeable effect on the"rising temperatures" 100 years from now, so 2030 is a ridiculous target.
3. There is another agenda behind climate change. Our job is to become aware of it and reverse this trend that will affect us much more than benefit us.

The countryside is not so bad after all

I MUST CONFESS, I have always been a city girl. I like to live close to restaurants, shopping possibilities, and entertainment. Coming from a densely populated city in Northern Mexico, it was unthinkable for me that one day I would see any advantages of living in the countryside. This view is changing now after many years living in Switzerland where you have easy access to forests, mountains, and many wide natural landscapes. I really appreciate living surrounded by Nature. It is an inspiration for me, and it has become a necessity to live around green areas.

This mindset shift about living in the countryside instead of big cities started during the COVID pandemic times. Being locked down in a small apartment in the middle of the city felt like being in a mousetrap. I'd never felt like that before, but it made me reflect on living in cities versus living in more open areas like in the countryside.

Looking at big cities like New York, Shanghai, Mexico City, and Paris, you realize quickly that the common ground is the gentrification and the over-crowded areas. The idea of living in the city as being "the cool thing to do" and a better place for living and finding work, education, and entertainment opportunities have pushed many people to move to the city from the countryside.

It has also brought many people from different cultures and nationalities together to create a "cosmopolitan" feel. To live in the center of a trendy city, people are willing to live in small, cramped, and very expensive apartments, just so they can live near a Starbucks.

This phenomenon has been one of the consequences of globalization. By standardizing big cities, bringing all the same big brands, the big commercial chains, and entertainments, people then feel attracted to them. It is like how honey attracts the bees.

In my opinion, this can also be a trap. Attracting people to big cities has been a big trend since the 50s, and the result is clear: overpopulated cities, pollution, high costs of living, destruction of local markets in favor of big commercial chains, and people becoming less communal, more selfish, isolated and self-serving.

Nobody realizes they live in a cage until they open their eyes and dare to see beyond the common ground. When cities were closed during COVID, and you lived in the middle of a big city, in a small apartment in a high tower, with no possibilities to do anything else since everything nearby was closed (bars, restaurants, cinemas) what was there left to do? It surely felt like all the people were trapped in square boxes without a piece of land to touch and feel. Without trees, flowers, and big horizons.

Being honest with myself, I came to the conclusion that living in a big city felt more like an ecosystem for insects and rats. It does not really fit with the territorial nature of humans. We don't like to feel squeezed in and live without horizons. To live in a small space in the middle of a city feels like a people-shelf, an anti-natural niche. A place for lost souls obliged to enter and exit through the same door.

That's when I realized that the countryside is not so bad after all. Owning your own piece of land, being able to own your own little garden, where you can actually grow your own food, seemed like a better quality of life.

To own your own place where nobody can tell you what to do, where there are no house rules, neighbor fights for laundry, timetables or noise, where the horizon is wide, the surroundings green, and the souls are free, where you can support a local farmer, where you can live in smaller communities where people look after each other, this standard of living was common before the World War II, only to become slowly obsolete as we were moved towards globalization and the global economy.

Now we are talking about "smart cities" and 15-minute cities. Not only are we becoming "trapped" in crowded areas, now the idea of some governments is to reduce your movements even more by restricting drive times to 15 minutes. A trip farther than that can incur fines or even prison. The governments are trying to sell the 15-minute city as a way to make cities "greener" but the essence of this book is to invite you to look further and ask yourself some critical questions about whether this initiative is based on well-intentioned governments that care a lot about the environment and your well-being, or if this is another move to gain more power and restrict freedom.

Let's take a recent example to explain what a 15-minute city would be. One of the pioneer cities that will test this initiative starting in 2024 is the city of Oxford in the UK. The council released a statement after receiving feedback from worried citizens concerned that this measure would mean an actual movement barrier, resulting in citizens being confined to a 15-minute perimeter.

The council responded that the traffic filters they planned to implement were "not physical barriers of any kind, but simply cameras that can read number plates (...), so if a vehicle passes through the filter at certain times of the day, the camera will read the plate, and if you pass the quote and get caught, you will receive a fine in the post."[3]

Okay, it is not a physical barrier, but a movement barrier nevertheless. The council further said that "residents of some of the surrounded villages will be able to apply for a permit to drive through the filters up to 100 days a year (two times a week) or residents living in Oxford city can apply for a permit to drive up to 25 days a year" (two times per month equivalent).

This might sound innocent and well-intentioned for the reduction of vehicle congestion, the environment, etc., but the real danger to me is that once we accept such measures, we are simply giving more and more power away to the government, and we lose more and more of our freedom of movement.

Unfortunately, Oxford is not the only city that wants to implement such methods. Cities like Paris, Barcelona, Buenos Aires, and Bogotá[4] are also considering the idea of becoming some of the 15-minute cities of the future.

I do not pretend to demonize the concept itself. It is an interesting idea to consider, having all the basic infrastructure reachable to you and within the neighborhood like your workplace, shopping, entertainment, convenience stores, etc. It is also quite naïve to think that the 15-minute perimeter infrastructure would benefit everybody. The danger is not in the fact that you live closer to convenience stores and your workplace; the danger is if they use this as an excuse to restrict movement based on "carbon emission concerns" or "climate change" or other such topics. I wouldn't trust anything that comes from the excuse of reducing carbon emissions or climate change: When I hear those two, I smell a hoax.

Most of us do not live close to our families. What if your parents live outside this 15-minute threshold? What if most of your loved ones live hundreds, or as in my case, thousands of miles away? Would there be restriction on seeing them based on "carbon emission measures"?

Apparently, only the carbon emissions of ordinary people is affecting the environment so much.

What about the tons of carbon emissions that were used up by private jets flying to the Qatar 2022 World Cup? Or during the World Economic Forum in Davos in January 2023? No, for those people, no restrictions exist whatsoever. They can fly in their private planes around the world, eat the most expensive meat in the world, have children, while lecturing you on how you should stay within a 15-minute perimeter, eat insects, not own a car, and not have children. That is the level of hypocrisy behind these initiatives.

That's why I don't find the idea of going back to the countryside such a bad idea after all. The idea of living freely, sharing the values of a true community, helping each other and looking after one another, looking at wider horizons and enjoying the tranquility and peacefulness of living close to nature in a more rural setting where mountains, flowers, and trees dominate the landscape instead of an endless pile of gray concrete and neon lights.

I certainly believe I belong in a rural community. When I was a child, I used to go to a small village called "El Yerbaníz." Back in the late 90s, this place became my second home during the summer, when I, together with my little brother and sister, escaped busy Monterrey so that we could spend the whole day riding our bicycles along the river, playing with the local neighbors until late at night, and enjoying that simple but beautiful tranquility of rural life.

It was idyllic. Why not live that way now?

Over-population or depopulation?

I HEAR IT EVERYWHERE: There are too many people on the planet. This, according to most governments, is an undesirable condition. When there are too many people, the Earth cannot provide enough resources. This "problem" gets addressed in all the world elite forums. King Charles of England said in one of his discourses at the G20 summit that "humanity's future is at stake if we don't act against climate change, especially in densely populated areas."

In our daily reality, we experience this "too many people" phenomenon on the streets, especially in big cities; everything seems to be overcrowded, traffic keeps increasing, you have to wait in long lines for everything and try to find a parking space! You might agree that, indeed, there are too many of us.

However, there is another reality that is becoming more and more apparent: we are really experiencing a population collapse.[5] Stephen J. Shaw is a prominent demographer who has observed a steep decline in birthrates, particularly in Europe, Japan, and the United States. He analyzed behavioral patterns in those countries and found that one of the root causes is the alarming number of women who remain childless during their reproductive lifetime.[6]

Of course, there are also many other effects in conjunction that make childbirth increasingly challenging, like the reduction in male fertility due to the dramatic drop in sperm counts, which is a global fertility crisis detected by Dr. Shanna Swan[7] who has been investigating this topic for the last forty years. There are also strong cultural implications, like society's emphasis on encouraging women to join the workforce, the emancipation of women's roles in society, and the gender equality movements.

According to demographic expert Stephen J. Shaw, the child rate threshold to sustain humanity is women having on average 2.0 children. Today, 70% of the world's population live in countries where the child-rate is below that threshold, mainly in the industrialized countries.[8] This will have profound implications in our societies, as the baseline of all civilization should look like a pyramid in order to sustain our current economic system and our sustained growth. If the pyramid gets inverted, collapse is inevitable.

The decline of the childbirth rate is one of the most fundamental social changes that are happening in human history; it is surprising how fast this transition is happening without the majority of people ever noticing. For example, it took China only 11 years to transition from 6 children to 3 children per woman before the one child policy introduced between 1978 and 1980. The fertility rate in 2023 was 1.7 children per woman, below the 2.0 baseline to sustain a balanced population growth.

Maybe it's time to open our eyes and become aware of the real depopulation crisis that will affect our world dramatically over the coming years. Do we stand a chance, or is it too late?

Time will tell.

For now, I want to introduce you to the last section of this book, and what I consider the most toxic ideologies of all: the idea of achieving progress through globalization and the "One World Government."

13. Toxic Ideology 5: Globalism And The One World Government

GLOBALIZATION... THE MOTHER OF ALL EVIL. I still remember how this concept of "Globalization and Free Market Economy" was being sold to us, or better said, being pushed on us through our education at schools, as the only way to progress. It all sounded very pretty: nations of the world can trade goods, services, labor, etc. and profit from each other's natural resources and talents.

Because of this tremendous shift from local to supranational economies, the world would accelerate its production and supply services and products to levels we have never been accustomed to. Then, global regulatory bodies emerged, like the World Trade Organization, established in 1995, conveniently just a few years before China signed a 1999 agreement with the United States to commit to adhering to the world trade rules under the WTO, which became "official" in 2001.

Then you had "Free Trade Agreements" between neighboring countries, and all sorts of international agreements that, basically, gave big corporations a bigger play-room to expand their sales and operations in markets beyond their current borders.

Before the big "boom" of globalization, most countries had a relatively strong workforce, strong local companies could supply regions with essentials. The nationally owned resources were consumed in the country, leaving the economic rewards in local society. But as soon as companies started to realize that they could profit from globalization, they started to shift labor from higher income countries to lower income ones to exploit the cheap labor and profit from the extra gains in capital.

Extracting the most profit from the most vulnerable economies became the standard business practice in global corporations. Let's take the textile industry as an example. Let's talk about Zara, founded by Amancio Ortega in 1975 in the city of Coruña, Spain.

Zara is an extremely popular, worldwide brand known for trendy, fast fashion clothes of regular quality. Although I must admit I like Zara and have bought products from them, it is also true that I have often wondered what makes fast fashion clothes so affordable and accessible to everybody. The idea of bringing fashion and design to everybody is not a bad idea, but we might not be aware of the real price we are paying when buying such clothing.

Being a global conglomerate, group Inditex (the corporate group of Zara), owns global supply chains that make those "cheap prices" possible. Perhaps, that cute top you bought on sale for $25 got the cotton and other raw materials from China, which cost just 1 or 2 cents, got dyed in Bangladesh by a woman who gets paid $2 a day for an eight-hour shift with no break, was transported in a big container that crosses the Atlantic Ocean for a few cents per ton, arrives by air at the nearest hub center close to your city, together with several more tons of clothes, and finally gets showcased in your nearest Zara shop.

The total production and distribution costs of that top for Zara might have been $5, which leaves Zara with a $20 profit, not bad for a company that sells 450 million items a year and makes over $13 billion in profits.[1] Does Zara really care about me and want to make sure I can dress nicely at an affordable price? Is that their only aspiration? Even if that means that their labor practices undermine the well-being of their workers, who have little choice but to work there?

And what about the waste and the toxic chemicals released into the water where the clothes dying takes place? Who is held responsible for destroying the lives of the people living in those rural communities, close to contaminated water canals where they get their domestic water? Is it worthwhile to pay $25 for a cute top made in Bangladesh, instead of paying $80 for a top made locally with local materials and decent paid labor?

It seems that with "globalization" we have no choice. Not many people can afford an $80 top just to support a local clothing company. Maybe because we are part of that cheap workforce as well! This thought scares me a little. But if we are honest about it, we allowed ourselves to become cheap labor the moment global corporations started to become more and more powerful and more effective at political lobbying. As a consequence big companies receive more protection from the government than ordinary citizens do, which leaves us with little power to defend ourselves against those "giants."

Globalization destroys the local economy

ONCE UPON A TIME, we had small local shops in our neighborhoods where we used to get most of our food and other necessities. I still remember when I was young, and well into the early 90s, my mother used to buy fruit and vegetables in a local "frutería" a few blocks away from where we lived. She used to buy meat in a local meat shop, bought freshly made tortillas in a local tortillería, and the rest we got in small pharmacies or "papeterías" close-by.

We rarely went to big supermarkets to do our grocery shopping.

Now that is all but a happy memory. Over the years, these smalls shops started closing one by one. Just about the time when big supermarkets like Walmart, H-E-B and others settled in the city. Now it is rare to find a small privately owned shop. And the few that still remain are being cannibalized by the convenience store chains like Oxxo's and 7-Eleven which are on virtually every corner in Mexican neighborhoods.

This makes me question who really benefits from this behavioral consumption change. If we go a step further and think about how rapidly online shopping has been growing, even the local physical supermarkets might not stand a chance in the future.

Amazon is the number one E-commerce platform in the world, with $514 billion net sales revenue in 2022, and this is projected to grow even more. According to the annual sales revenue shown by Statista,[2] Amazon's sales revenue has grown exponentially since 2019, specially between 2020 and 2022 when the revenue grew, in North America alone, from $170.77 billion in 2019 to $315.88 billion in 2022—an increase of 85%!

No wonder the world leaders call this era the "Fourth Industrial Revolution," the era of the digital world, where robots and Artificial Intelligence will replace not only the boring, repetitive, manual jobs, but also what we used to call more complex or sophisticated jobs like physicians, nurses, managers and even chefs, musicians, painters, and writers.

Unfortunately, I am not exaggerating. I read an article in *China Daily* that stated a Chinese robot became the first machine to pass China's national medical license examination, which is an essential step for aspiring doctors. Now, in the province of Hefei, Anhui is considering running pilot projects to see how these robots can assist doctors in real medical cases.[3]

Another sad example is that there are already some restaurants that use robots to cook and prepare the dishes with zero human interaction. A French robotics company has claimed to have created the world's first autonomous pizza making robot, Pazzi. It claims to make 80 pizzas per hour![4] They have also opened the first fully automated restaurant, where you can order and get your pizza delivered without the need of talking to anybody. You can check them out at Pazzi.com.[5]

I am sure there are many robot aficionados who find these advancements amazing and even think we are taking a step further in the advancement of our civilization. But I am not so sure about that. First of all, there are currently no global policies setting clear limits between our human sovereignty and the robot's capability to overrule our human condition.

What is more frightening is that I don't see any priority being given by governments to regulate the use of artificial intelligence. There have even been discussions about merging humans with machines. Many "futuristic" leaders in different fields have expressed excitement around implanting chips that could link directly to the human nervous system and establish a communication with a robot via the Internet.[6]

My question remains: What is the future of all this? What will it mean to be human, given those terms?

The global sociopath, technology philosopher and historian Yuval Noah Harari has a very clear picture of how the future of humanity might look like in the new world. He firmly believes that new technologies such as AI and Virtual Reality will at one point "outperform" humans in most of the daily tasks and as a consequence put hundreds of millions of people out of the job market, which will then bring the problem of creating a class of "useless people."

His philosophical worries are what to do with those people who are basically "useless" and "hopeless." His best guess, he says, is that those worthless people will spend their useless days entertaining themselves with a mixture of drugs and video games until the day they die.[7,8]

What a wonderful future, globalism, combined with advanced technological achievement will bring us, isn't it? The sad part is that this is no longer the future; it is happening now. Over the past few years, I have been monitoring the development of important cities around the world, and the prophecy of Mr. Yuval Harari is becoming true.

Major beautiful Western cities which used to be the cornerstone of prosperity are on the bridge of collapse, not only economically, but also on a social level. Cities like Los Angeles, Washington D.C, San Francisco, Vancouver, or even idyllic cities in Europe like Rome or Paris, are suffering a staggering rise in homelessness, drug addiction, and an increase in violence and crime.[9,10,11,12]

Globalization is going after the complete dominance of our economy on material terms. I dare say that the end goal is to merge humanity with AI and convert our souls and sovereignty into sellable products and an instrument of control for the governments.

Some people might think I am exaggerating and taking things too far. But I have been observing the development of this over the years, and while the majority of the people are busy with TikTok, Hollywood, and Facebook, governments like Chile are passing laws like the new "neurological rights," a project that makes possible the modification of the current Constitution to protect what they call the "rights over the brain" or "brain rights."[13]

So, what does that new law mean? It means that in order to protect your "mental integrity," the state has the right to record your mental activity and to own it. That's right, the state will become the official owner of your thoughts and mental activity. But don't worry, it is for your own good!

The idea to have something close to a law to protect the sovereignty of my thoughts and mental activity goes beyond me. I cannot understand how we have come this far. On the other hand, we have been allowing this to happen. We have built our own prison, and now we have to live in it.

Just think about how AI has become possible. Is it because some geniuses developed it "out of the blue" inside their garage? Where does AI get all the human intelligence data from? Maybe, maybe from social media? From the cookies installed in your computer which basically store all your activity?

Has it happened to you, that you have been thinking about buying a jacket for winter, and then when you open Facebook, you receive sponsored ads featuring jackets? It can be quite scary, but it is nothing new that social media and companies like Apple and Microsoft collect our personal data in many different ways. It always makes me smile, when a person tells me: "Oh, Paola, I forgot my iPhone! I feel so empty, my whole life is in that phone!"

I cannot help but thinking: "And the iPhone owns your life, too!"

Globalization and culture

IF YOU ASKED ME what my favorite thing about traveling is, I would definitely think about the cultural uniqueness of a place. One should not travel just to see another beach, or another building. Places have a rich historical and cultural context that makes it special. You do not go to Paris just for the sake of seeing standard buildings and eating hot dogs. You go to admire the architectural beauty of its buildings and monuments; to see the iconic Eiffel Tower, to experience Parisian culture, to try the original Parisian baguette, to marvel at the Louvre Museum.

Well, my friend, let me tell you the bad news: if we continue with the current rates of globalization, all that will be left in Paris will be McDonald's, Starbucks, Zara, and iPhone stores. Every time I travel to a remote place, like Japan, South Africa, or Korea, it amazes me to see how the uniqueness of the culture is becoming less and less apparent.

People, especially the younger generations, all look exactly the same, everywhere you go. They all wear jeans, use an iPhone, go to Starbucks, wear the same fast-fashion brand and watch the same Netflix movies. The only remaining things to see that are different are historical monuments and relics in the museums. There may be some regional restaurants, but these are becoming the exception and not the norm.

Another thing I used to collect, and I found very precious, was the local currencies. Bills or coins from that specific country. Now, with the introduction of digital money and "cashless" payment terminals, you barely need to get any cash.

It is my personal observation, but I see a danger in globalization damaging the structure and culture of countries worldwide. The domination of global brands and a global culture will definitely destroy local traditions and cultural heritage at some point.

As a proud Mexican, I have sadly seen how this trend is transforming Mexico. From being an extraordinary country with vast cultural richness and historical heritage, and being home to the Mayans, one of the greatest civilizations in the history of humanity, and being host to more than 80 different indigenous languages, I watch with sadness as the current government treats those national treasures as "tourist attractions" and gives more and more value to modernism; building huge shopping centers, opening more and more American fast-food chain restaurants and the like.

Preserving local cultures and traditions has always been very dear to civilizations until the early 19th century. But something happened during the 20th century that accelerated the modernism as a consequence of globalization. Traditions became antiquated and old-fashioned, and modernism became the novelty and the trend. When searching for the meaning of "modernism" I found an interesting description in the Oxford Dictionary. The first says "Modernism is a style or movement in the arts that aims to depart significantly from classical and traditional forms." A second definition states that "Modernism is a movement towards modifying traditional beliefs in accordance with modern ideas, especially in the Roman Catholic Church in the late 19th and 20th centuries."

You can also see the effects of modernism in the latest architectural tendencies. Talking about the Catholic Church, just look on the Internet at how churches are being built today versus centuries ago. You might be very surprised, just like I was. For me, it was horrifying to see the modern designs. They are not only simpler and uglier, but also quite scary in their appearance. They look more extraterrestrial. Their shapes do not fit at all with the image of real beauty, in my opinion.

Of course, it is also a matter of taste and perspective, but I don't like them. For example, check out the Cathedral of St.Mary of the Assumption in the United States, built in the late 70s, or the Parish Church of Santa Monica,[14] built in the early 2000s, located in the south of Madrid, Spain. Now, compare those churches with the Chapelle Notre-Dame in Paris, built in the 13th century, or the Florence Cathedral, built in the 12th century, majestic buildings with exceptional beauty and splendor. You can see and feel the Glory of God represented. Not anymore in the modern ones.

The famous Argentinian author Agustín Laje argues in his book *Generación Idiota* (*The Idiotic Generation*) that, in modern societies, adults are being pressured to act like teenagers and the children to act like adults. This is reflected in how an adult has to be constantly entertained, like if boredom means something is wrong with your life. An adult today cannot sit in peace. They have to be constantly stimulated and entertained, otherwise they feel anxious and depressed. Adults in today's world are hypersensitive, overstimulated, weak, confused, and lack a proper set of fundamental values. Reality is subject to any personal interpretation.

On the other hand, children are being pushed to become aware of their sexuality through "education" in very early days. Many schools are also teaching small children about "gender neutrality" and LGBTQ rights. How can small children be confused about their sexuality?

As a mother of two wonderful kids, my experience has been that if you allow them to be free, they intuitively choose their male and female roles, even with no intervention from my side. My daughter loves pink and princess dresses, and my little boy loves cars and fire trucks. Kids have a pure soul and a very positive and loving view of the world. In the eyes of children, you see God. Their purity is sacred and must remain sacred. Powerful institutions know this and know that kids are the greenest of fields to impose ideologies on that can destroy their souls.

I don't believe in coincidences, nor in the fact that "society itself" pushes for those ideologies. I believe we are being pushed, and we are merely complying with an invisible agenda, where we have no say and no vote.

To recap the effects that globalization has had on our latest generations, I will quote the lyrics of the song "Degeneration" from the iconic Quebecois band, Mes Aieux:[15]

Your great-great grandfather, he cleared the land
Your great grandfather, he plowed the land
And your grandfather made the land profitable
Your father sold it to become a state employee
As for you, my boy, you don't know what you're gonna do

*In your small one bedroom, way too expensive, too cold in the
winter
Now you would like to become a landowner
And during the night you dream with your own plot of land
Your great-great grandmother had fourteen children
Your great grandmother had almost so many
Then your grandmother said that three were enough
Then your mother did not want to have any, you were an
accident
And now you, girl, you change partners all the time
When you do something stupid you end up with an abortion
But there are mornings where you wake up crying
When during the night you dream a table full of children
Your great-great father lived in misery
Your great grandfather saved every penny
And then your grandfather became miraculously millionaire
Your father inherited it and invested all in his retirement
And now you, youngster, you owe your ass to the Ministry
You cannot hold a single dollar in the bank
And when you feel like robbing the cashier
You calm down reading about "voluntary simplicity"
Your great-great parents know how to party
Your great grandparents danced strongly in parties
Then your grandparents knew the ye-ye period
Your parents the "disco guys" met at the disco
And now you, my friend, what are you doing at night?
Turn off the TV, there is no need to be stuck on the couch
Luckily, there are things in life that never change
Get your nicest clothes, that tonight we will dance."*

Small is beautiful

I MUST ADMIT that after seeing what globalization has
done, not only to our planet, but to civilization, I can only
conclude that small is beautiful. Globalization promised
"unlimited economic growth" but at what cost? And who is

really benefiting from this growth? Clearly, not the environment; also not the so-called "poor countries" which are used just to extract natural resources from them, or dumping tech trash on them, with complete disregard to the people actually living there. It's the big industries and their lobbyist institutions and governments who are really benefiting from it.

Globalization has made our trade economy cheaper, faster and more scalable. This has also brought changes in behavioral consumption. People want everything fast, one-day deliveries, instant gratification. The joy of craftsmanship and conscious production of something is losing its meaning. Creating something used to be of great pride and cherished just some decades ago.

Countries proudly used their "Made In" signature, especially if coming from a high-quality product. Switzerland used to be proud of the precision of their "Swiss watches." With the Made In America cars, and Japanese TVs, the "Made In" was a symbol of being proud of your craftsmanship and expertise. Nowadays, everything is made in China or Bangladesh. When we take away this human element, the fact that products were made with care, with regard and with consciousness, then it just becomes a "thing." It's a piece of plastic or metal, which has some use, but you can dump it just as easily.

A fully tailored, hand-made dress will have a completely different meaning to you than a cheap, mass-produced dress from Zara. With the latter, you will feel not sorry to throw it away after some use. A hand-made dress, on the other hand, you would want to keep forever. The problem is that thanks to globalization, ordinary people can afford less and less to have a tailor-made dress and must conform with the cheap mass clothing from their favorite fast fashion store.

Big corporations control the supply chain worldwide to make sure they can squeeze the most profits. It is all about decreasing production and shipping costs and increasing the profit margin.

Yes, I have been working many years in big and medium corporations, and I can tell you, this is all that matters.

Of course, the idea is not to demonize industry and prosperity. Industries, when growing at a proper rate, can be very beneficial for local communities if they are able to provide jobs and improve living conditions of the place. What we should be careful about are the big corporations, the ones that grow at uncontrolled rates, and end up monopolizing the economy.

Just remember what happened during the pandemic. When local businesses had to close and go on forced lock down, many went out of businesses or had to ask for huge loans to survive. On the other hand, big companies with global online platforms became the absolute winners. As I mentioned previously, companies like Amazon, Facebook, Microsoft, etc. all tripled their profits because people could not go out and buy locally.

Taking away the pure profit view, we should look back to what makes an economy great. Economy is a human activity. It is the capability to create and share our creations, to grow at an organic rate, in tune with nature. It is to get back to having dignity and joy of producing, and not just become a rat trapped in a small cubicle looking at a screen all day long creating Excel sheets and making difficult phone calls.

I like these wonderful words by Fritz Schumacher, economist, journalist and author of *Small is Beautiful*: "Above anything else, there is a need for a proper philosophy of work which understands work not as that which it has indeed become, an inhuman chore as soon as possible to be abolished by automation, but something as decreed by Providence for the good of man's body and soul."[16]

14. Toxic Ideology 6: The One World Government

I KNOW THIS TOPIC has caused much controversy. The idea of a one world government is the target of many conspiracies. The idea of finding "global solutions to global problems" has been sold to us intensively since World War II with the establishment of the United Nations (UN), but many of us were not aware of it, because we didn't have the technology providing the instant news that we have today.

The intention of the establishment of one world government became more obvious to me during the pandemic. Karl Schwab, founder and executive chairman of The World Economic Forum, wrote in his book *COVID-19: The Great Reset*,[1] that crises like the COVID-19 pandemic were the consequence of national governance failures and a lack of a coordinated global response.

He exposes in his logic that this "highly interdependent and interconnected world" (caused by globalization, by the way) needs to get out of their "silo thinking" (a.k.a. your national sovereignty). He continues by saying that "The containment of the Coronavirus pandemic will necessitate a global surveillance network capable of identifying new outbreaks as soon as they arise."[2]

Well, here I challenge Mr. Schwab in his statement that countries were not "coordinated" enough during the outbreak.

At least the hospitals and governments seemed very much coordinated when telling us which variants and which segments of the population were most at risk, reported by the news media with impressive precision, as I mentioned in the first chapter in the section "Chronicles of a Pandemic."

Not only did Mr. Schwab enthusiastically support global surveillance, but also did most Western governments. We heard multiple times how Prime Ministers like Justin Trudeau in Canada or the ex-Prime Minister Jacinta Ardern in New Zealand, or American President Joe Biden would claim that the world problems of "climate change," "COVID" or the "Ukranian war" required a coordinated global response and was the opportunity for a "global reset."

And of course, there are those global institutions like the World Economic Forum (WEF)[3] which has the mission of "engaging the foremost political, business and other leaders of society to shape global, regional and industry agendas"; the "Global Governance Project" which report on what the Group of Seven (G7) and the Group of Twenty (G20) submits. The Heinrich Böll Stiftung Institute[4] defines the G-groups as "homogeneous, intimate groups which have been meeting for decades (...) to discuss issues of global importance."

As though those were not enough, we also have global institutions like the United Nations (UN), the World Health Organization (WHO), and the World Trade Organization (WTO) which have a big influence in shaping country policies, even if their nature is "non-profit" and "nongovernmental."

If you observe what has been going on in the world, particularly since the start of the 21st century, the speed at which changes are happening has gone completely insane.

The events of September 11, 2001 were the start of a series of wars and economic crises and astonishing advancements in technology that, when I look back, make it difficult to recognize the world anymore.

At the turn of the 21st century, we had only just started using cellphones, and back then, there were no colorful displays or smartphones. The electric car was nowhere to be seen, and although the Internet was gaining popularity, there were no such things as big social networks, no YouTube, no TikTok or the like. People still got the news from newspapers or the TV.

Twenty-four years later (2024), we are talking about ChatGPT,[5] which is an artificial intelligence chatbot developed by the OpenAI company. It is an impressive algorithm that is able to compute vast amounts of knowledge and mimic human conversation, and according to the other features offered, it is also capable of writing essays, computer programs, compose music, tell fairy tales, write poetry, etc.

ChatGPT has many competitors, with a continual jockeying about which AI is more capable and creative. Elon Musk's X has its own called Grok, and he naturally believes it is best. Given the reach of his social media platform, he may end up being correct.

Perhaps Mr. Yuval Harari was not so wrong in his "predictions" in his book *Sapiens: A Brief History of Human Kind*[6] when he predicted the end of Homo Sapiens once we are able to engineer completely inorganic beings like computer programs, capable of self-learning and self-evolution. That would mean that computer programs allowing machine learning could learn anything from driving cars, playing chess, cooking, managing projects, composing music, etc., and eventually, will outperform "old-fashioned humans."

Most of those technological advancements are heavily supported by governments around the world. Canada, for example, plans to invest $30 million in AI in robots, according to an article in IT World Canada.[7] The European Union is investing one billion Euros in the Human Brain Project (HBR), one of the top EU research projects that aims to employ supercomputers to reconstruct a human brain and use it to control robots and to test drug treatments.[8]

It sounds like science fiction, but it is our new reality.

"Any intelligent fool can make things bigger, more complex and more violent. It takes a touch of genius—and a lot of courage—to move in the opposite direction." ~ E.F Schumacher

"The improver of natural knowledge absolutely refuses to acknowledge authority as such. For him, skepticism is the highest of duties; blind faith, the one unpardonable sin." ~ Thomas Huxley

Part Three
The Truth Will Set Us Free

15. The Origins Of Evil

WE HAVE THE NOTION as humans that we are intrinsically acting with two main powerful energies, the ones we call "the good" which is the energy we use when doing things we regard as positive, orderly, peaceful, loving and meaningful, and we also operate with "the bad" that is negative energy where we focus more in what favors evil: hate, violence, division, chaos, fear, cowardice.

Evil is nothing new for us. It has been with us since the beginning of times; the Bible refers to it as the original sin in the Adam and Eve story; ancient cultures and mythologies all around the world speak of demons and angels.

I have been aware of the good and evil forces that surround me in my life. But for some reason, during my daily routines, I have noticed that when it comes to interacting with our communities, and in recent times when we follow public discussions, the narratives from the mainstream media outlets follow a very clear trend in which sort of energy they broadcast.

It might be subtle, even unrecognized by most people, but this energy is right there, going into our conscious and unconscious mind... the narrative telling us about a chaotic, unpredictable world... a dangerous world, full of wars, dangerous viruses mutating from nature itself, and climate change caused by the same filthy, irresponsible people.

It is this constant storytelling of "you humans are bad, you are doing everything wrong, the world is on the verge of collapse because of your greedy, stupid actions, you should be ashamed of yourself" in fact, that has made it totally okay nowadays to get an abortion, or to confuse your children about their gender.

Those media outlets, the prominent voices of our times, are spreading, in front of our eyes, rhetoric with totally negative energy. The messages are destructive, negative in nature, and depressing at best. And the worst part is that it is not really the truth of what people really are. Neighbors willing to help. Families that are longing to raise their kids in peace, harmony and prosperity. My personal conclusion is that people, when they think and act rationally, do not want to harm nature, nor other people. Most people want to live in peace and do not like conflict. We all regard health, love, security and peace as highly valued treasures to defend.

I do not know which sort of people those media outlets are referencing. I refuse to believe that evil comes from the real essence of humanity. The Bible emphasizes that we have been created by God in his image. That was the real meaning behind sending his Son, Jesus Christ, to show us that we have been created just like his Son, and in that sense, we all are the children of God.

So, where are these evil forces coming from, and why has humanity been suffering from the influences of these forces? I do not want to speculate, but after doing my own research about it, I have the conviction that the source of evil is not human in nature. In fact, it is a force that goes beyond our spans of human rationality and physical reality. When I started to dig into this topic, I came across Salvador Freixedo, who was a Spanish Catholic priest and ex-member of the Jesuit order. He has written several books about the relationship with religion and paranormal activities and the possibilities of extraterrestrial activities happening on our planet. One of his last books, called *Teovnología, el origen del mal en el mundo* (*Teovnology, the origin of evil in the world*) claims that, in fact, we are just a human herd, belonging to other beings that are the real owners of the world.

Yes, I know that with that statement I entered the realm of conspiracy and madness. Our whole life, we have been instructed (I don't know by whom) that we are the "kings" of the world, because of our intelligence, and our ability to dominate over the animal kingdom. But for some reason, even if we are the kings of the world, we simply struggle to relieve ourselves of our miserable fate of pain and suffering.

The other day I read a small quote from an interview with the prominent Spanish writer Antonio Gala. The interviewer asked Gala, "Mr. Gala, what is the smartest thing that someone can do with their lives?" to which Gala responded: "In the beginning, I would tell you: Go to the beach. But in reality, I have to tell you that the best thing to do is to get out of this rabbit hole in which we have been condemned, in a life that is not really ours, and which is not the one that is meant to be."

"This is an organized prison which needs slaves to keep operating as a prison and it is so until the end. You have to break the chains, even if you risk being alone, to get exposed to a lack of understanding, but get away to the forest, in the best of senses. Get out of this monotonous daily slavery. Give to each day its own smile, its own essence and its own joy. That is real intelligence. Because the type of intelligence that does not help us to live, is not worth it, I don't want it. I don't think it has worth to anybody".

I got chills through my spine while reading this simple but powerful statement from Gala. Are we living in a prison, without us even realizing? Who is pulling the strings from above?

Of course, I am not referring to the obvious, to the extremely corrupt elite and weak leadership that is apparently "leading us" from the surface. There must be a more powerful source that is really pulling the strings.

16. Freedom Of Expression: Our Most Powerful Tool Against Evil

THERE WAS ONCE A TIME I believed I was free. That I had free will over basically everything I was choosing in life. Besides my childhood, when I could not influence many of the events, since I took consciousness of choice, I thought all my decisions were fully mine.

Little did I know that all the information I had access to was already molded and filtered in a way that fits to the current societal realities and ideologies. I was also ignorant of the huge amounts of money and great efforts in propaganda made by governments and other "higher" organizations to suppress people who had a different, rebellious opinion about how things work in the world. Our minds and opinions were profoundly manipulated from the shadows, but ordinary people like me had been completely ignorant of it.

What chance was there that we could question ourselves whether something was true or not? I guess most people rarely questioned the media. What we saw on the news, on the mainstream TV channels, in the newspapers and magazines must be the truth, no?

From all the illusions I had about life, the one that hurt the most was to learn that we are born, destined to be subjected to all sorts of lies and manipulations. The indoctrination starts very early in life, from the moment you innocently join kindergarten, which is literally the official indoctrination to the "current society." In our world, there is very little tolerance for being truly free and having freedom of expression. I think this is where we fight between Heaven and Hell.

The fear and anxiety of existence prevents us from choosing freedom over control. When we feel afraid or insecure, we prefer that other people choose for us instead of taking full responsibility of our thoughts and actions. Victimhood is deeply rooted in our belief that somebody else should take responsibility from our personal life. It's like never growing up. Staying childish, fragile and weak forever.

Humanity has always been repressed. Jesus Christ was killed because the Jewish authorities and their temple could not tolerate the truth, and they were afraid to lose their power once people found out that the Son of God was among us. We destroyed our own Savior and have been negating Him and His Love ever since. Every time we lie. Every time we choose force instead of real power. Every time we hurt children. Every time we choose fear over love.

We have recently observed a controlled demolition of the United States, which used to be one of the freest countries in the world. The United States Constitution is considered one of the most wonderful political documents.[1] It has endured two centuries, and in our 21st century it is being threatened by a government populated by people who have extreme left, communist ideologies.

The beauty of the Constitution is that it claims that the truth is self-evident: that all men are created equal, that they are bestowed by God with certain unalienable rights, that among those are Life, Liberty and the Pursuit of Happiness.

And very importantly: That to secure those rights,

governments are instituted among men, deriving their limited powers from the consent of the governed.

Looking at the state of affairs in the United States since 2022, it seems hard to imagine that such a document, which is considered the supreme law of the country, is even being taken seriously.

It is also worrisome to see how Christianity has been declining over the last few decades.

CBS news published an article that projects that Christianity will no longer be the majority religion by 2070. According to the Pew Research Center, in the 1900s, about 90% of U.S. adults were Christians. In 2007, that number became 78%. In 2022, it fell even further to 64%. On the other side, people that have "no religion" has increased from 16 to 29% since 2007.[2]

Why are we losing faith in God? Why should a predominantly Christian country make such a shift in faith?

Inherently, there is nothing wrong with changing religion or not having a religion. But that's not the point. The point is that Christianity as a form of religion is under attack by communist governments that know that such faith empowers individuals to pursue the virtues of the religion, which is based in freedom, love, and compassion. And by the way, not only is Christianity under attack, all forms of religion are under attack.

Remember the "holy war" against the Middle East back in 2003? Remember when all Muslim-like people were considered "terrorists" in America after the September 11 attacks? Actually, I'm not a fan of the church and its corrupt modus operandi. Religion as ideology has been used as a powerful tool of oppression and manipulation for centuries. But it is also true that the values on which the essence of religion stands is for pursuing the highest of good, which undermines the current fear mongering agenda of the oppressors.

I could make a long list of examples of how we are being

threatened if we say our own opinion or express our rights freely. For starters, look at the amount of censorship existing in social media today. Just to give you a taste of it; after Elon Musk bought Twitter, Apple threatened to take the app out of the Apple Store for not censoring accounts that might be compromising China by exposing videos of the absolute repression that their citizens are living in since the pandemic.

Remember how the Twitter account of Former President Donald Trump was suspended minutes before the supposed "violence riot" which broke out in the White House back in January 2021? After taking over the platform, Musk restored the account of Trump, based on a poll where Twitter users could vote whether the account should be restored or not. With a majority of votes (ca.51%), Musk announced "Vox Populi, Vox Dei" (The voice of the people is the voice of God).[3]

David Icke, one of the most popular voices among the "Renegades," a man who has been exposing the hidden agenda of the New World Order and the Illuminati for decades, has been banned from mainstream media, and even today he does not even have the right to enter European Union territory (being himself British by birth), because he is branded as "a conspiracy theorist, bringing hate speech and antisemite messages." He does none of that. But he does bring awareness to people about the current state of the world, to transform woke with awake. He has written brilliant books like *The Trigger*, which exposes the whole September 11 lie, and *The Biggest Secret*, which exposes the dark side of the royal families, elite politicians, and big industry cartels. If you are curious about his work, you should definitely check out his books. You can also follow him on X @davidicke.

We don't need to live in China or North Korea to realize that even though those countries are the extreme examples, everywhere in the world, freedom of expression is a rarity and not the norm. As I discussed in the section of the book dedicated to political correctness, the groupthink tendencies of the societal constructs leave very little space for authenticity, individualism, and true creativity.

The pursuit of the truth is a God-given duty, and to really get on the pathway to the truth, you need to follow your heart, respect your individuality, and grow self-confidence in your divine origins. That's why, as a human endeavor, the search for the truth is one of the most difficult but more sublime duties we will ever have.

We have the power within us to change the course of our destiny as humanity. We can get out of the trance and wake up to a new reality. One of the first steps to doing so is to do our uttermost to preserve the truth at all costs. And I suspect the very first step is the most difficult of all: Embrace telling the truth and stop lying.

17. In A World Full Of Lies, Have The Courage To Speak Your Truth

I f the devil has a home, it must be built of lies.

Language is possibly one of the most powerful tools for survival in our human arsenal. Only through language is it possible to live in communities, form entire civilizations, and transcend the animal kingdom by being able to convert an idea into matter through the explicit use of words.

We create our own world, but we rarely think about the mechanisms of how precisely we are building that world for ourselves. How can we shape our own life?

The answer that came to my mind is simple: through language.

Language is so powerful, so magnificent, that it can create wonderful things as much as it can completely destroy them. By the use of language, you are crafting your life... word by word. So, what happens when you use your language to distort reality?

We know that we can say anything we want, and we shape our own reality by doing so. That's why lying is considered something regular people do most of the time.

Everybody tells a lie, here and there, right? It can be a white, non-offensive lie, or a big one.

As Joseph Goebbels, the sinister politician of the Nazi

era used to say: "If you tell a lie big enough and keep repeating it, people will eventually come to believe it."

If the critical mass of people believe the lies and regard them as true, big lies can become collective realities. A collective lie which is seen as reality can define the destiny of entire nations and the world at large.

Lies can be powerful allies when you want to hide from someone or something. Telling lies is a defense mechanism to avoid facing and dealing with the truth... with the pure and naked reality. In that sense, it is logical to think that the more you lie, in order to get certain things in life (maybe power, money, recognition, acceptance... whatever it is) the farther away you are from knowing your true self.

Liars get lost in a thousand-mirror puzzle. One little lie has to be covered by a bigger lie, and the bigger lie by another very big lie, and if you are not clever and keep track of all the lies, you will start to contradict yourself; you will lose your sense of reality. You will be disoriented and out of touch. You will probably need to invent a new lie to get out of that embarrassing situation, but it will be a weak foundation and will collapse again once you have to cover up the new lies associated.

What a strange world. Why do we ever rely on lies to live our lives? Lying builds sand castles with unstable foundations, but telling the truth really keeps you firm on the ground.

Real and deep human interaction that is constructive only comes from a place of trust. And to be trusted, you need to tell the truth. Here's how you can start practicing getting your true voice out:

When you talk, pay attention to your inner emotions.

- Do you feel nervous, or inadequate, or does your voice sound weak? If that's the case, you are talking from a place of fear, which is fertile ground for lying.

- Start to consciously recognize your own lies; every time you catch yourself saying one, write it down and keep a log; are you capable of doing such an exercise?
- When you are caught telling a lie, ask yourself: What will be my expected benefit for having said that lie? What could be the consequence if I ever got caught? What result has more impact on my life and why?
- If you want to discover who you really are, ask yourself: Am I willing to pay the price of knowing who I really am? Even if that means being exposed to my own truth, my authentic thoughts and desires? Am I willing to defend myself by always striving to tell the truth?

People demand constant communication to keep their minds organized. Therefore, by communicating with the language of truth to others, you are not only helping your own mind come to terms with your true self, but you are also helping others to do so as well. Because as much as lies are contagious, truth is even more potent. People recognize the spark in the eyes, the passion that emanates from the eloquent, honest heart.

18. We Must Preserve Families At The Heart Of Our Civilization

HEALTHY FAMILIES represent healthy societies. In healthy families, the mother and father role are of primary importance, and they have different, unique responsibilities. The mother provides the "nest" filled with loving care and protection. Mothers also have the primary role of raising children. The father has a strong assertive figure. The father provides food and shelter, and protects his family against potential danger.

There is more than enough evidence that dysfunctional families are the major source of violence in young adults. Candace Owens, a popular voice in America in favor of the Black community, posits that the number one problem in the black community is a lack of fathers in the home.[1] She is not the only one raising this concern. It comes from studies made back in the 60s where economists were already warning about the dangers of dysfunctional families.

The main consequences of growing up without a father at home are increasing probabilities of kids dropping out of school, the increasing likelihood of ending up in poverty, and the higher probability that those kids end up committing crime.

In America, it is estimated by the Center for Disease

Control and Prevention that around 70% of children in black families are born without a father. This is an alarming number and worth being worried about. I read an article in an online Spanish magazine which stated that around 25 million kids in America are living without their father at home.

This is a tendency that is growing not only in America, but worldwide. In Europe, around 16% of European families are composed of a single parent, 83% of those have the mother as the single parent, according to recent statistics published by Eurostat.[2]

It is clear that the more we support single family setups, the "empowerment" of women, meaning that we give praise to strong, emancipated woman who can handle it all and do not need men, the more we are pushing away the male figure and taking away his fundamental role in society. Not only that, we are also destroying the mother figure in a way that pushes kids away from their parents and into the hands of "institutions" that indoctrinate them. The State becomes the big father.

Just think about how society praises the emancipated woman today: in the super skinny and perfect body of models and athletes, there is no place for a baby. There is no time in the busy schedule of the businesswoman to take care of a child, nor do the glamorous lives of artists and most celebrities have space for changing diapers and living a boring, routine life of raising small children. As a young girl, I had that inner desire to be a mother. I liked to play with baby dolls and carry them around as if they were my kids. I fantasized about forming a family. But as I grew up, more and more female "role models" were imposed on me by society.

As a result, I felt guilty for wanting to be a stay at home mom, because that is not cool, you are not generating value in the capitalist society.

In the society I grew up in, you are destined to be

judged regardless of the choice you make. If you chose to be a mother and stay home to raise your kids, you were seen as "opportunistic and lazy." If you decided to make a career and not have children, you were judged as "weird." If you did both, you were called "greedy." Nothing we ever do will please society. And maybe that's the goal: without solid families with clear roles of male and female figures, no family can thrive.

Families are the pillar of our civilization, because that's where it all starts. It is your mother and father who teach you values, clothe you, and provide a warm nest where you feel secure. Without this warm loving nest, what is left?

That's why I am a firm believer that we must protect the traditional family construct. We must fight against everything that might threaten it. Family is the only social group where people are really willing to die for the other. Families need a common vision to stand for; without the family construct, we don't have a core, and something without a core or a basic strong foundation will collapse over time.

19. Education Is An Operation Of The Soul

ONE OF THE MAJOR PILLARS in any civilization, from the past and for the future, relies on the art of education. Education, in Latin "educatio," means directing or guiding, and "educere" which connotates "revealing" or "exposing" to the outside. In ancient Greek methodology, in the schools of Socrates and Plato, education was not only a practical duty, but also a spiritual one. It was not only relevant to learn about astronomy, mathematics, geometry and history, it was also critical to examine one's life in light of the philosophical and religious torrents of the era.

Education took various forms and shapes during the centuries, but it wasn't until the 18th century that the concept of a "public standardized education" started to take shape. John Taylor Gatto, American ex-professor and author of *Weapons of Mass Instruction*,[1] cites in his book a famous professor, Arthur Calhoun, who said that after World War I ended in 1919, many utopian enthusiasts started to see the possibility of bringing one of their wildest dreams to life: "children passing from blood families into the custody of community experts," which would provide fertile land for manipulation and population control.

Gatto also alludes to the claims that the Ex British

Prime Minister Benjamin Disraeli made a few years before the explosion of "compulsory schooling" back in 1920. Israeli claimed that "all important events were controlled by an invisible government, of which the public was unaware." We are talking about the beginnings of the 20th century. Apparently, many people back then were aware of the existence of this "invisible government" and about the plans of controlling human behavior, and ultimately, the control of human life.

These facts are shocking, and many would consider them exaggerated; but looking how the world is today and what education has become in the 21st century, I believe that such plans have been executed with remarkable precision. Education today has nothing to do with the integral development of human wisdom and the human soul. It has become a rather mechanistic and pathetic template of contents to standardize the level of "knowledge" of individuals, but with high emphasis toward the agenda of industrialization and scientific rationalization of human affairs. A system that has nothing to do about education, but indoctrination.

When I joined university, I remember looking at all the potential "professional careers" one could choose from in elite universities. The type of careers that were most popular were the ones that would allow you to join the workforce: management, engineering, finance, sciences, etc. There were few choices when it came to philosophy, arts, religion, and history. Even if there was an offer, those type of careers were not popular because one "cannot make a living out of them."

These academic agendas, which, incidentally, nobody knows from where they come (ahem... Rockefeller Foundation, anyone?), have been totally destroying the illusions of many kids and teenagers since the beginning of the 20th century. Many of us have heard stories like: The prominent artist who ends up studying medicine because his parents told him that he cannot survive by painting. Or the gifted guitarist who had to abandon his passion as a hobby because he needs to work as a cashier in some random store to earn a living.

Charles Bukowski, the prolific American writer and author of the popular novel *Post-office*, portrays very well how broken the system is; unable to work as a writer, he portrays his life in a cynical, brutal and sometimes sad way; his broken dream to live his life as a writer was replaced by alcoholism and shitty jobs to get by. In an ideal world, this would be just a fictional character. The reality in our times is worse beyond imagination. In 2022, there were more than half a million homeless Americans, including families with children.[2]

Sometimes, I wonder how this life would look if our educational institutions had never been corrupted to such a profound degree? Imagine, just for a second, that education belongs back with the individual and with the communities where one belongs. Imagine all your glorious childhood years spent exploring in the forest, playing, in a self-directed and self-meaningful way.

How society would look when each of us has the power to lead his or her life on their own, following the real school of parental and family values and traditions. How many hours, days, months and years does a young soul not get to enjoy the sunlight of a summer day because she has to be locked down between four walls learning some compulsory bullshit no one, not even the teachers, care about.

Education is a matter of the soul. Education is not limited to some set of skills and standardized knowledge that help you land a job. As Gatto wrote in his amazing book, the current education system is systematically designed to make it difficult for people to maintain control over their own thoughts and opinions.

20. Education And Technology

THE TECHNOLOGICAL ERA and the dumbing down of our educational systems came in "handy" for the 21st century. With the mounting technological revolution, communication, and basically the way we interact and do our affairs, has changed dramatically. Now everybody has a laptop and a smartphone, which keep you connected 24/7 to the Web.

The simplest acts like writing by hand, doing multiplications with your hand or mentally, is becoming completely obsolete. Nowadays, you can use the calculator integrated in your iPhone, or even ask "Alexa" to do it for you. Not only is what we are learning in schools severely manipulated and designed to keep us "stupid," now it is not even necessary to make an effort.

The younger generations do not need to make the effort to learn anything like that. Memorizing the multiplication tables is a thing of the past.

It turns out the brains and souls of our young generations, the ones that grew up in the 2000s and later, have been kidnapped by the social media era—the era of the idiots. I like the concept of Agustín Laje, author of *Generación Idiota*[1] about the nature of the idiot; coming from the Greek word "idiotes" where "idio" means "self" and "tes" means "without the agent or influence." So basically, idiotes is someone that is self-centered and does not have a "public opinion" or does not really understand what is going on around them. We can see this behavior very prominently in our younger generations today. They are mainly selfish, hedonistic and self-centered.

But there is an even more interesting definition which increases the scope of the idiot, posited by Laje, inspired by Ortega y Gasset;[2] "the massified idiot." Basically, the massified idiot is someone who is not only uneducated about the world that surrounds them; but believes that their opinion, which is often misinformed, unstudied, shallow, and predictive, is as valid as others.

The massified idiot is the typical person who listens to what mass media says and, if it becomes trendy, this individual perpetuates the narrative and accepts those facts as truth without question or further study.

If the narrative fits with their own self-centered attitude, it even becomes a morality. With the emergence of social media, this behavior can be seen everywhere. Topics like climate change, the Russia-Ukraine war, the COVID narrative and many other man-created crises had a specific narrative that became the "massified version" of the facts. People who vehemently think that carbon dioxide kills whales, and Putin is the root of all evils, are a typical example of a kind of person that supports an opinion without any other solid foundation but an intoxicating need to feel self-righteousness and popular.

When the massified idiot joins public opinion, this becomes quite dangerous. It threatens the real, honest aspiration of the search of truth. For the narcissistic, massified idiot, only their own version of the truth is the one that is real. The equality and inclusion agendas introduced recently in many schools and academic institutions allow for distortion of logic and truth by protecting "everyone's backgrounds, feelings and personal orientations."

In my opinion, education is the greatest gift to our species. Our ability to learn from our environment and the capability to build solid relationships with one another has made us the most advanced species in the world. But even beyond learning how to navigate our physical reality, education also has another dimension: the education of the soul.

Our soul, on its deepest level, knows the truth, because our soul is our direct connection to God. God gave us the light of reason so that we can understand his teachings, which are displayed in all natural laws that govern our existence and in the highest virtues that are taught to us through the arts, philosophy, even religion, or the texts that serve as inspiration to pursue religion, like the teachings of the Bible.

Education was not meant to be something that "I had to be forced to learn" just because someone told me that this is what I should study. I reflect on what Gatto considered to be a crisis in education back during his time as a teacher in the late 90s. He argues that his biggest worry is that education in the 2000s looks exactly the same as it did in the 90s and the 70s. Even if we go back to the 1800s, education has not varied much in form, content, and format.

If we go even further back, let's say the 1700s, there you can really see a difference. Back then, it was possible to become very educated, because there was no time extraction of the young from family life, nor imposed servile habits on the growing up of kids. There was also no indoctrination in centralized camps, where they have to bear the burden of learning pre-thought thoughts.

The whole practice of having to start at the age of four or five to follow a strict attendance schedule, filled out by a pre-thought academic "plan" all serves for what? After one century of being in this schooling system, where everything is standardized and way too many people want to push you to learn from them, I believe we are in a worse position than ever. The new digital generations have no patience and no resilience to endure the long path of education; they want to get everything quick and easy, watching YouTube videos, checking posts on social media, and finding immediate answers to their questions by searching with Google.

The rigorous, long and often painful task of research, observation, and understanding are becoming obsolete. Now "viral" and "immediate gratification" have become more important than true knowledge.

21. How To Embrace The Return Of Real Education

GOING BACK to true education requires that society re-thinks the meaning of education. True education means, in my opinion, to train your thought process to become aware of your environment and surroundings. To understand the past and previous achievements and failures of civilization in order to understand the present and plan for the future.

Education should evolve according to one's own hard-won personal blueprint of value instead of judging education levels based on standardized tests or memorizing external opinions.

The biggest value of education comes from recognizing that all work, including creative expressions, are based on the highest virtues of Love, Justice, Respect, Curiosity, Reverence, and Empathy. The curiosity to learn and understand the operations of life in order to be able to serve good to others; to become a benefit to humanity, and not a disturbance or a burden.

This real value is not rooted in material wealth. One of the big burdens of our civilization has been the idea that education is only a tool to get more money or to earn a living and even as a "means" to get rich.

We have placed too much importance on money, financial markets, Wall Street, banks and institutions that, as a matter of fact, have been systematically helping the rich to get richer and making the poor poorer. I am by no means a financial expert or an investment guru, but I have studied and observed the financial crisis over the years and the easy money scheme, especially in America, where there is a Federal Reserve "place" or "institution" that is private and that nobody knows how it became so powerful, but somehow has the power to print money without limits and inject capital every time Wall Street has a crisis, keeping interest rates low so that industries and people have the illusion of being able to afford things when in reality... there is no substance to it. From one moment to the other, the "Fed" increases their interest rates and Bang! It destroys the economy. Suddenly, companies cannot pay their debts, which are quite illusory, because they were generated from thin air to more thin air. "Electronic money" they call it.

Anyway, my intention is not to discuss the questionable practices and motives of those financial institutions. Something that is very clear to me is that a well-educated civilization would have been informed enough to take appropriate action and avoid such tyrannies to begin with. Only, we are not educated. We are indoctrinated, and we are trained to see reality as taught at school, without knowing that we are actually living in a world of illusions.

22. We Must Preserve Our Historical Heritage

I DON'T KNOW ABOUT YOU, but I think that, in our postmodern era, nobody cares about history. What matters today is the instant, the moment, the viral news... nobody dares to look back, not even a few years ago in time. All the political movements happening today, like climate change, for example, are rooted in people's ignorance and inability to remember the past. People buy the propaganda of the moment.

If Greta Thunberg tells me that the previous generation is responsible for the melting of the ice poles, it must be true. If Black Lives Matter tells me that white people are evil and black the eternal victims, and you saw a documentary on Netflix or a Hollywood movie that backs up that claim, then it must be true. This simplistic, often incomplete judgement of present events just reflect our profound ignorance, and maybe our lack of interest in the past.

To dig into and understand our history requires a lot of time and a targeted effort to connect the dots of historical events and its consequences. Many of the feminist enthusiasts who blame the current patriarchal and machismo cultures forget that this "patriarchal, repressive" society has made it possible to preserve our civilization up to today.

People supporting abortion practices, LGBT rights, emancipation of women, etc., forget that we need kids to preserve humanity.

People that judge religion and attack the Christian Church, the Muslim Church, or any other religion, forget that the church is the only institution that has kept virtue and moral values alive for thousands of years. The malpractice of the church might be self-evident, but we cannot deny that the fundamental teachings are still rooted in doing the highest of good.

The inhumane conditions imposed on us during the COVID era is a clear example of how easy to manipulate we are, and how quickly we forget our recent history. Just 80 years before, we suffered from the terrible Nazi era and World War II. The same segregation method used against the Jewish community back then was used against the nonvaccinated in the COVID era. The green pass is the present representation of the Jewish star in Nazi times. The concentration camps built to hold people who had a "positive COVID test" or mandatory self-imprisonment at home. It is almost surreal to think that 80 years have passed, and we have learned absolutely nothing from history.

In a way, it is not entirely our fault. There are so many things that "mainstream knowledge" has kept hidden from us, from our own human history. Unfortunately, many of us will never know to what extent our history has been a series of manufactured events, or real events manipulated in a way to fit certain interests. When I say such statements, people often tell me that believing that a worldwide event can be manufactured is "too simplistic" because of the "complexity" of the world.

For me, complexity is nothing else but a lack of understanding. What we do not understand, we automatically label as "complex." It is "too complex" to understand the Russia-Ukraine war. Too complex to understand the propagation of deadly viruses. Too complex to understand how the war created such a huge financial crisis worldwide. Those events are too complex for little people like us, so governments know best how to handle "complexity" with simple explanations.

This is the explanation that Kamala Harris, Vice President of the United States and Democrat candidate for President in 2024, the highest ranked woman (of color, sorry) in America, offered when she got asked about how the war would affect Americans: "Uhm so, Ukraine is a country in Europe, and it's next to another country called Russia. Russia is a bigger country and more powerful. So, Russia decided to invade the smaller country called Ukraine, so that's wrong."[1]

Yep, I'm not making this up. Apparently, a normal, unimportant individual has to pursue years and years of education and even get doctorate degrees to ever make it somewhere close to a high rank position... and if you think government is doing something evil, or attempt to criticize them in any way, then you are branded as just too stupid or simply do not understand the world. But Ms. Harris doesn't need any of that. She solved the problem of explaining the reason for the war.

Thank you, Ms. Harris, for your unlimited wisdom and incredible intelligence that allows you to decipher the war in such an elegant manner. Now it is time to go and get myself a new electric car, become transgender, eat insects, and keep paying my taxes so you can use my money to buy more weapons for Ukraine because they do not have enough, such a small country. My country can collapse, I might not be able to pay the rent tomorrow, there might be no money for my healthcare, and I might end up in the street, but it will all be worthwhile, because we are helping little country Ukraine against big country Russia.

I truly believe that if you really want to understand our current world events, you have to do the research on your own, and we definitely need to understand and study our past. Not trusting all the information "thrown at you." You must remain critical and question the logic and substance of events. We should bring back the respect for our history, and our history is best transmitted by our elderly, our museums, our art, historical buildings, monuments, and books. There is so much mystery, so much knowledge hidden to mankind. In the search for truth, one must invariably look at the past to understand why we are where we are today.

Matt Walsh, a popular right-wing political commentator in America, could not have said it better: "Progressivism is the religion of self-hate. It teaches the whites to hate their skin color, the children to hate their sex, the woman to hate their feminism, the patriots to hate their country and the West to hate their history. What a horrible and toxic ideology it is."

23. The Kingdom Of God Is Within

"But if I cast out the devils by the Spirit of God, then the Kingdom of God is come unto you" - Matthew 12:28

WAKING UP HURTS, but it's a good sign. The biggest motivation for writing this book was simply to share my own path to the greatest spiritual awakening of my life, after having lived all my life in a state of illusion, where it was very difficult for me to imagine that the battle of good and evil was being fought not only in an allegorical way in front of my eyes, but also that the enemy began to attack me from the first minute I was born on this Earth.

The existence of evil has always been based on man's weakness; we all have the ability to agree to do good or do bad. Where Satan's trap resides is in the inverted system in which he operates; it creates a world of mirrors, where what is good seems bad, and what is bad seems good. A clear example is the emergence of toxic ideologies that damage common sense and the use of reason, which are very important instruments when it comes to seeking the truth and, above all, connecting with God.

Toxic ideologies and oppressive political regimes operate at very low vibrational frequencies, where basically fear and rejection of human dignity are the main drivers of their modus operandi.

The problem of humanity is that we have lost the course that led us to God, to the divine, to the good, to the just, and to the truth, and we are losing ourselves in an abyss turned into progressivism, an uncertain future with no clear vision. Is our future self-extinguishing for not learning from our mistakes? Will we ever be able to get out of the woke trance we have been in throughout recent decades? Will artificial intelligence completely replace us? Will the world of the future be inhabited by an army of robots serving a handful of elite beings?

Could it be that we are approaching the end of times, which the Bible predicted would be 7,000 years after the cataclysm caused by Adam and Eve?

If so, at least we have the consolation that the return of Jesus Christ is near, or so the Bible says. Since no one knows exactly when it will happen, or if it will ever happen, it is up to us as humanity to fight this battle well. This world, with all its tragedy and malevolence, is our home, and it is where our next generations will live. We have to work collectively, striving to do good, give our best effort, and follow God's teachings to recover our freedom, our dignity, and our sense of existence.

Not so long ago, I read another interesting interpretation of the return of Christ. Dolores Cannon, the famous regressionist, addresses this topic in one of her books *The Convoluted Universe, Part 1*. In one of the sessions she conducted with one of her subjects, it was revealed by a channeled entity that the return of Christ had already happened, and that he exists among us today. However, it is not in the form we always imagined, which is incarnated in a single person form. The channeled entity reveals that the return of Christ came in several people, born in Christ's spirit. In fact, billions of people around the world today have the spark of Christ within.

Although this is thought-provoking, it goes in line with the key messages of the Bible which teaches us that the kingdom of God is within. The explanation is that if all humanity comes together in one mind, then that would be equivalent to the return of Christ.

Although this idea goes against traditional beliefs and the religious status quo, I think it is worthwhile to open our minds to new possibilities and ways of thinking. If we are all interconnected, and if we share the same cosmic destiny, then it is not completely crazy to think that if we all unite in love and increase our vibrational energy to higher levels, then we could reach higher levels of awareness and energies that are currently out of our reach; and we could eventually reach the highest levels, reaching Christ energy.

Dr. David R. Hawking,[1] a renowned American psychiatrist, physician, researcher and author, developed the widely known "Map of Consciousness" which was the result of more than forty years of work, clinical tests, and studies he performed in the attempt to understand the physiology of the nervous system and its holistic relationship with the human organism.

His discoveries led him to build a map of the energetic nature of human consciousness that he could base on specific conscious-based processes like emotions, perceptions, attitudes, visions of the world, and spiritual beliefs.

Based on his map, the lowest level, which is represented by an LOC (Level of Consciousness) logarithm of 20 or lower, experiences mainly humiliation, and seeks to self-destroy itself. It touches the emotion of shame surrounding human nature, and has the vision of God as being derogatory, and life is perceived as miserable. Then, those levels of consciousness that go in the scale from misery to hate, start to become a turning point at 175 when we arrive to the levels of pride and eventually courage in our emotional scale.

Courage (LOC 200) is, according to Dr. Hawking, the critical point where our vibrational energy and level of consciousness start to bring positive and strong energies, which then start to bring positive emotional states and higher levels of awareness about reality.

Levels of 500, for example, represent, in Hawking's scale, the love and the raising of an elevated spiritual consciousness; Levels 700 to 1,000 reach the vision of God as one, with the one that IS pure consciousness and complete illumination. It is said that Christ calibrated at 1,000 LOC as well as other avatars like Krishna, and Buddha. This is the highest level of divine grace ever known by humanity. If you are interested in seeing the scale of consciousness by Dr. Hawking, I have added it in the Appendix at the end of the book.

Knowing that we have the means to calibrate our electromagnetic radiation and map it based in our emotional scale gives me interesting evidence to believe that, indeed, it might be extremely rare to come up with a single individual that calibrates 1,000; but the collective sum of all calibrations of all humans on earth might one day come collectively to that level.

In our current society, that seems extremely difficult to accomplish. According to Dr. Hawking, the collective human consciousness is at a Frequency between 150 and 200. This is also mentioned by Christina von Dreien,[2] a young Swiss woman who was born with a greatly expanded consciousness, capable of handling multiple paranormal events such as multi-dimensional perception, connection to higher dimensional spheres, and clairvoyance, just to mention some. Her book, named *Christina*, is mind-blowing to read, and it opened my view to so many unknown territories that I had been totally unaware of. Christina believes that the collective consciousness of humanity is rising, and that there are already new generations of children being born with much higher awareness, capable of bringing more enlightenment to the world.

This leads me to believe that, even for non-religious people, it is clear that to experience love in a more conscious manner should be our ultimate goal. Wars, crises, famine, misery, fear, and hopelessness belong to the lowest of our emotions and bring the worst out in us. We become our own victims and, whether caused by our own lower nature or by ignorance, this becomes fertile ground for evil energies to take control of us and manipulate us.

I don't know about you, but I find it difficult to imagine that the levels of evil that currently exist are only human in nature. After reading the work of a good number of researchers on the subject of UFOs and interdimensional beings, among whom I recommend reading Salvador Freixedo, Graham Hancock, and Dolores Cannon, I am leaning more toward the idea that evil is mostly imposed on humanity, only when individuals operate in lower vibrations are their plans successful.

In the Bible, there is talk about the existence of "angels" and "demons" whose interpretations could very well be attributed to beings of light and beings of the shadow. Good entities like "The Guardians" or fallen angels like the Nephilim.

Regardless of whether you agree or not that there are other entities that inhabit the Earth and govern us, what is left for us to do? What can we do today to fight back?

I believe that a first step, perhaps the biggest of all, is to wake up to the reality that evil has ruled the world for thousands of years. And that, in recent times, it manifests itself in a more shameless, more accelerated, and more aggressive way than before. That is why we live in critical times in the history of humanity. Does it have a relationship with the urgency of implementing Agenda 2030? Better to remain critical about it and question everything now, and not fall prey when it will be too late to escape.

This is a call, an invitation to reflect on life's true meaning and become aware. Will we continue to allow humanity to head toward the ultimate destiny of slavery–a destiny planned by the fallen angels? Or will we wake up and fight against our eternal oppressor and allow the raising of collective consciousness to bring us to a higher vibrational frequency, one where beauty, justice, truth, love, and peace become our ultimate goal and destiny?

Our entire civilization depends on it. God is with us.

THE SPIRIT OF GOD IS UPON ME

The Spirit of the Lord Yahweh is upon me!
Yes, Yahweh has anointed me!
He has sent me his good message for the humble, to announce to the exiles their liberation, and to the prisoners their return to the light.
To publish the year of favor of Yahweh,
The day of our God's revenge, To comfort those who cry and give them a crown instead of ashes, the oil of happy days, instead of mourning clothes, songs of happiness, instead of mourning."
- Isaiah 60:61

"Our whole knowledge of the World is in one sense, self-knowledge."
- Alan Watts

About the Author

Paola Knecht is a leadership & transformational coach, and author. The founder of My Mindpower Coaching & Consulting, Paola is dedicated to helping people improve all areas of their lives. After working more than fifteen years in global renowned companies, she decided to give a complete shift to her life and do what she really cares about: to become an author and help people all around the world to find their personal life's meaning through coaching.

She lives in Switzerland with her husband and two children.To follow for upcoming publications, visit her author webpage:

www.paolaknecht.com

Appendix

The map of consciousness from Dr. David Hawkins

Vision about God	Vision about life	Level	Logarithm	Emotion	Process
Be	Is	Illumination	700-100	Inefability	Pure consiousness
Omniscent	Perfect	Peace	600	Extasis	Illumination
One	Complete	Joy	540	Serenity	Transfiguration
Loving	Benign	Love	500	Reverence	Revelation
Wise	Significant	Reason	400	Comprehension	Abstraction
Merciful	Armonious	Aceptance	350	Forgiveness	Trascendence
Inspiring	Hopeful	Willpower	310	Optimism	Intention
Facilitator	Satisfactory	Neutrality	250	Trust	Liberation
Permisive	Feasible	Courage	200	Affirmation	Empowerment
Indifferent	Demanding	Pride	175	Contempt	Arrogance
Vengeful	Antagonist	Anger	150	Hate	Agression
Negative	Dissapointing	Desire	125	Compelling desire	Slavery
Punitive	Terrorific	Fear	100	Anxiety	Retreat
Disdainful	Tragic	Grief	75	Regret	Discouragement
Condemner	Desperate	Apathy	50	Desperation	Resignation
Rancorous	Malign	Blame	30	Blame	Destruction
Despective	Miserable	Shame	20	Humiliation	Elimination

Source: Hawkins, David. El Poder frente a la fuerza: Los determinantes ocultos del comportamiento humano

Appendix

(Spanish Edition) (p. 73). El grano de mostaza S.L.. Kindle
Edition.

Recommended Lectures

If you want to explore more deeply the topics addressed in this book, I highly recommend the following readings:

1. Ether, God and the Cosmic Superimposition - Wilhelm Reich
2. Grain Brain: The Surprising Truth about Wheat, Carbs, and Sugar - Your Brain's Silent Killers - David Perlmutter
3. Diabetes without Problems: The control of diabetes with the help of the power of metabolism (Spanish Edition) - Frank Suárez
4. Staying alive - Vandana Shiva
5. 1984 - George Orwell
6. Ten Arguments for Deleting Your Social Media Accounts Right Now - Jaron Lanier
7. Ship of Fools: How a Selfish Ruling Class is Bringing America to the Brink of Revolution - Tucker Carlson
8. 12 Rules for Life - Jordan B. Peterson
9. Blackout: How Black America Can Make Its Second Escape from the Democrat Plantation - Candace Owens

10. The Parasitic Mind: How Infectious Ideas Are Killing Common Sense - Gad Saad
11. The Trigger: The Lie That Changed The World - Who Really Did It and Why - David Icke
12. The Biggest Secret: The Book That Will Change the World -David Icke
13. False Alarm: How climate change panic cost us trillions, hurts the poor and fails to fix the planet - Bjorn Lomborg
14. Small is beautiful - E.F Schumacher
15. Spiritual Secrets Revealed - Raimon Samsó
16. Weapons of Mass Instruction - John Taylor Gatto
17. Dumbing Us Down: The Hidden Curriculum of Compulsory Schooling - John Taylor Gatto
18. Idiotic Generation: A critique of adolescentism (Spanish Edition) - Agustín Laje
19. Power vs. Force: The Hidden Determinants of Human Behavior (Spanish Edition)- David Hawkins
20. The Convoluted Universe Part I and II - Dolores Cannon
21. Christina, Twins Born as Light - Bernadette Von Dreien (Only available in German)
22. Modern Man in Search of a Soul - C.G. Jung
23. Teovnilogía: The Origin of Evil in the World (Spanish Edition) - Salvador Freixedo
24. The Human Farm (Spanish Edition) - Salvador Freixedo

Afterword

I would love to know what you think of A World Of Illusions.

You can write a review at the social platforms below or write me a personal note at info@paolaknecht.com With your review, you help me enormously to learn what you love and what you don't, so I will be able to write better books for you!

- In the platform you got the book
- Facebook/Instagram - Search Paola Knecht
- Goodreads - Search Paola Knecht

Follow me on the socials:
Instagram: @paolaknecht_author
X: @PaolaKnecht

References

1. What We Learned About Health Is Wrong

1. Swissinfo (27 April 2021): Alternative medicine no longer an 'Outsider' in Switzerland's health system: https://www.swissinfo.ch/eng/society/ going-mainstream_alternative-medicine-no-longer-an--outsider--in-switzerland-s-health-system/45706024
2. Reich, Wilhelm. Ether, God and the Cosmic Superimposition. New York: Farrar Straus and Giroux, 1973
3. Eccles, John C; Popper Karl. The self and its brain: an argument for interactionism. New York: Routledge, 1983
4. Reich, Wilhelm. Ether, God and the Cosmic Superimposition. New York: Farrar Straus and Giroux, 1973
5. C.G Jung. Modern Man in search of a soul. New York: Houghton Mifflin Harcourt, 1933
6. American Collegue of Orgonomy (11 November 2022): Wilhelm Reich https://www.orgonomy.org/reich.html-
7. Note: The orgone accumulator was a six-sided box constructed with multiple layers of organic materials which served to attract the energy, and also used metallic materials to radiate the energy to the center of the box. Patients would sit inside the box to absorb the orgone accumulated.
8. Peter G. Peterson Foundation (23 August 2022): Why are Americans Paying More For Healthcare? https://www.pgpf.org/blog/2022/02/why-are-americans-paying-more-for-healthcare

2. We Are What We Eat, But What Are We Eating?

1. Most produced crops in the world (2021): Sugar cane, Maize, Rice, Wheat, Potatoes, Soya beans, Cassava, Barley – Source: Statista (2021):
   Production volume of the most produced food commodities worldwide in 2021, by product, https://www.statista.com/statistics/1003455/most-produced-crops-and-livestock-products-worldwide/
2. Shiva, Vandana: Staying alive. Berkeley, California: North Atlantic Books 3rd Edition, 2016
3. Healthline (23 August 2022): Experts Agree: Sugar Might Be as Addictive as Cocaine https://www.healthline.com/health/food-nutrition/experts-is-sugar-addictive-drug#What-is-an-addiction

References

4. Elite Medical center (6 September 2022): How Sugar Affects Children, https://elitelv.com/how-sugar-affects-children/
5. NHS (6 September 2022): Which foods cause tooth decay?, https://www.nhs.uk/chq/pages/which-foods-and-drinks-containing-sugar-cause-tooth-decay.aspx/amp/
6. World Crunch (6 September 2022): Not 'Lovin' it! Brazilian Parents Want Ronald McDonald Out Of Their Children's Schools, https://worldcrunch.com/culture-society/not-039lovino39-ito39-brazilian-parents-want-ronald-mcdonald-out-of-their-childreno39s-schools
7. BMJ Nutrition Prevention & Health (2022): McDonald's seems to be focusing on kids in lower-middle income countries, social media post suggest,https://www.bmj.com/company/newsroom/mcdonalds-seems-to-be-focusing-on-kids-in-lower-middle-income-countries-social-media-posts-suggest/
8. Perlmutter, David. Grain Brain: The Surprising Truth about Wheat, Carbs, and Sugar - Your Brain's Silent Killers. Hodder & Stoughton. Kindle Edition, 2014

3. Chronicles Of A Pandemic

1. Forrest, Adam (17 June 2021): Coronavirus: 'Exponential rise' in Covid cases in England driven by younger people, https://www.independent.co.uk/news/uk/home-news/covid-cases-england-young-people-b1867611.html
2. Stone, Will (1 May 2021): COVID 'Doesn't discriminate by Age': Serious Cases On The Rise In Younger Adults. https://www.npr.org/sections/health-shots/2021/05/01/992148299/covid-doesnt-discriminate-by-age-serious-cases-on-the-rise-in-younger-adults
3. El Pais (2021): Spain reports new rise in coronavirus infection rate as cases among young people continue to spike, https://english.elpais.com/society/2021-07-02/spain-records-new-rise-in-coronavirus-infection-rate-as-cases-among-young-people-continue-to-spike.html
4. CNN (March 2021): Los casos de covid-19 en jóvenes están aumentando en Brasil, según un informe, https://cnnespanol.cnn.com/2021/03/30/brasil-jovenes-casos-covid-19-aumentan-trax/
5. El Economista (2021): Incrementan los contagios Covid-19 entre los jóvenes en América, alerta la OPS, https://www.eleconomista.com.mx/internacionales/Incrementan-los-contagios-de-Covid-19-entre-los-jovenes-en-America-alerta-la-OPS-20210505-0049.html
6. ABC News (2020): Melbourne aged care is facing a coronavirus catastrophe. This is how it happened, https://www.abc.net.au/news/2020-07-29/victoria-coronavirus-aged-care-outbreaks-timeline/12498532
7. World Economic Forum (12 March 2020): An expert explains: how to help older people through the COVID-19 pandemic, https://www.

weforum.org/agenda/2020/03/coronavirus-covid-19-elderly-older-people-health-risk/

8. Orwell, George. 1984 . HMH Books. Kindle Edition.1977
9. Eurostat (2022): Excess mortality hits +16%, highest 2022 value so far   https://ec.europa.eu/eurostat/web/products-eurostat-news/-/ddn-20220916-1
10. MDPI (2022): A case Report: Multifocal Necrotizing Encephalitis and Myocarditis after BNT162b2 mRNA Vaccination against COVID-19, https://www.mdpi.com/2076-393X/10/10/1651
11. Kirsch, Steve (2022): Vaccine adverse reaction articles, https://stevekirsch.substack.com/p/vaccine-adverse-reaction-articles
12. React 19 (2022): 3400 COVID Vaccine Publications and Case Reports,https://react19.org/1250-covid-vaccine-reports/
13. Crow, James (2002): Unequal by nature: a geneticist's perspective on human differences, https://www.amacad.org/publication/unequal-nature-geneticists-perspective-human-differences
14. Biology online (2022): Living Things Definition, https://www.biologyonline.com/dictionary/living-thing

4. Naïve Childhood

1. Los Angeles Times (2021): Opinión: A 27 Años del asesinato de Colosio, siguen las dudas, y otra vez me vino el recuerdo de Mario Aburto, https://www.latimes.com/espanol/mexico/articulo/2021-03-23/opinion-a-27-anos-del-asesinato-colosio-siguen-las-dudas-y-otra-vez-me-vino-el-recuerdo-de-mario-aburto-al-recuerdo
2. Contra la corrupción (2020): Los expedientes secretos del caso Colosio, https://contralacorrupcion.mx/colosio/evidencias-fotografias/

5. The Illusion Of Having A Life On Social Media

1. Lanier, Jaron, Ten Arguments for Deleting Your Social Media Accounts Right Now. Henry Holt and Co. Kindle Edition, 2018

6. The Other Side Of Feminism

1. Friedan, Betty. The Feminine Mystique. Penguin Modern Classics, 1963
2. Carlson,Tucker. Ship of Fools: How a Selfish Ruling Class is Bringing America to the Brink of Revolution. New York: Free Press, 2018
3. The General Social Survey (2021): About, https://gss.norc.org/About-The-GSS
4. The National Wildlife Federation (2021): Mallard, https://www.nwf.org/Educational-Resources/Wildlife-Guide/Birds/Mallard

5. Peterson, Jordan B. 12 Rules for Life. Random House of Canada. Kindle Edition, 2018

7. The Career Illusion

1. National Bureau of Economic Research (2009): The Paradox of Declining Female Happiness, https://www.nber.org/system/files/working_papers/w14969/w14969.pdf
2. Owens, Candace. Blackout: How Black America Can Make Its Second Escape from the Democrat Plantation (p. XV). Threshold Editions. Kindle Edition.

8. Going Back To Basics

1. YouTube (2023): Jordan Peterson - How Society Brainwashes Women, https://www.youtube.com/watch?v=ud6y1bMLyDg

9. Toxic Ideology 1: White Supremacism

1. UNAM MX (2022): Los Pueblos Indígenas de México, https://www.nacionmulticultural.unam.mx/100preguntas/pregunta.php?num_pre=4
2. Saad, Gad. The Parasitic Mind: How Infectious Ideas Are Killing Common Sense. Washington: Regnery Publishing, 2020
3. 9/11 Memorial & Museum (2022): World Trade Center History,https://www.911memorial.org/learn/resources/world-trade-center-history
4. Icke, David.The Trigger: The Lie That Changed The World - Who Really Did It and Why, Derby, UK: Ickonic Publishing, 2019

10. Toxic Ideology 2: Gender Equality And Transgender Movements

1. Forsey, Caoline (2022): Gender Neutral Pronouns: What They Are & How To Use Them https://blog.hubspot.com/marketing/gender-neutral-pronouns
2. Hawkins,Derek (2021): A professor was reprimanded for refusing to use a transgender student's pronouns. A court says he can sue. https://www.washingtonpost.com/education/2021/03/27/transgender-pronouns-shawnee-state-professor/
3. The New York Times (2023): Heavily Armed Assailant Kills 6 at Christian School,https://www.nytimes.com/2023/03/27/us/nashville-shooting-covenant-school.html

4. California Courts (2023): The Gender Unicorn, https://www.court s.ca.gov/documents/BTB25-5I-oI.pdf

11. Toxic Ideology 3: Political Correctness

1. YouTube (2023): Lopez-Mirones, Fernando. El Mono Egoísta, https://www.youtube.com/watch?v=os-tZFtbISI
2. National Geographic (2022): Key Components of Civilization, https://education.nationalgeographic.org/resource/key-components-civilization
3. Swissmedic (26 August 2022): Reports of suspected adverse reactions to COVID-19 vaccines in Switzerland, https://www.swissmedic.ch/swissmedic/en/home/news/coronavirus-covid-19/covid-19-vaccines-safety-update-17.html

12. Toxic Ideology 4: Climate Change And Over-Population

1. Lomborg, Bjorn: False Alarm: How climate change panic cost us trillions, hurts the poor and fails to fix the planet. New York: Basic Books, 2021
2. AG Daily (2022): New Dutch emission rules hamstring farmers & threaten food security, https://www.agdaily.com/news/dutch-emission-rules-hamstring-farmers-food-security/
3. Oxfordshire County Council (2022): Joint statement from Oxfordshire County Council and Oxford City Council on Oxford's traffic filters, https://news.oxfordshire.gov.uk/joint-statement-from-oxfordshire-county-council-and-oxford-city-council-on-oxfords-traffic-filters/
4. Deloitte (2023): 15- Minute City, https://www.deloitte.com/global/en/Industries/government-public/perspectives/urban-future-with-a-purpose/15-minute-city.html
5. World Economic Forum (2021): Bye, bye baby? Birthrates are declining globally - here's why it matters, https://www.weforum.org/agenda/2021/06/birthrates-declining-global-fertility-decline-empty-planet-covid-19-urbanization-migration-population
6. Shaw J, Stephen (2022): Brith Gap - Childless World Documentary https://www.birthgap.org/spaces/10215679/page
7. Swan, Shanna H; Colino, Stacey (2022):Count Down: How Our Modern World Is Threatening Sperm Counts, Altering Male and Female Reproductive Development and Imperiling the Future of The Human Race, New York: Scribner, 2022
8. Roser, Max (2023): The decline of the number of children per woman since 1950, https://ourworldindata.org/fertility-rate

13. Toxic Ideology 5: Globalism And The One World Government

1. Beeketing (2023): How Zara sells out 450+ million items a year without wasting money on Marketing, https://beeketing.com/blog/zara-growth-story/
2. Statista (2023): Annual net sales revenue of Amazon from 2006 to 2022, by segment, https://www.statista.com/statistics/266289/net-revenue-of-amazon-by-region/
3. China daily (2023): Chinese robot becomes world's first machine to pass medical exam, http://www.chinadaily.com.cn/business/tech/2017-11/10/content_34362656.htm
4. Artificial Inteligence (2022): Pazzi- The World's First Autonomous PizzaRobot, https://www.aiplusinfo.com/blog/pazzi-the-worlds-first-autonomous-pizza-robot/
5. Pazzi Robotics (2023): Pioneering robotics in restaurants, https://pazzirobotics.com
6. Warwick, K. (2015). The Merging of Humans and Machines. In: Londral, A., Encarnação, P., Rovira, J. (eds) Neurotechnology, Electronics, and Informatics. Springer Series in Computational Neuroscience, vol 13. Springer, Cham. https://doi.org/10.1007/978-3-319-15997-3_6
7. Youtube (2023): Yuval Noah Harari, How Drugs & Video Games Have Been Instrumental in Controlling the Population, https://www.youtube.com/watch?v=VZP5lIzGNT8
8. Morgan, Jacob (2022): Yuval Harari on The Future of Jobs & Technology, Intelligence vs Consciousness, & Future Threats to Humanity,https://thefutureorganization.com/yuval-harari-on-the-future-of-jobs-technology-intelligence-vs-consciousness-future-threats-to-humanity/
9. Sjostedt, David (2023): Plan to Solve Homelessness in SF Is Unfeasible, Says Department Tasked With Doing It, https://sfstandard.com/public-health/homelessness/plan-to-solve-homelessness-in-sf-is-unfeasible-says-department-tasked-with-doing-it/
10. Euronews (2023): Homelessness and poor quality of living is on the rise in France, https://www.euronews.com/2023/02/01/homelessness-and-poor-quality-of-living-is-on-the-rise-in-france
11. CTV News Vancouver (2022): Most B.C residents says homelessness a major problem, governments doing bad job addressing it, https://bc.ctvnews.ca/most-b-c-residents-say-homelessness-a-major-problem-governments-doing-bad-job-addressing-it-1.6035242
12. Seckin, Baris (2022): 'Invisible' owners of streets and squares in Italy: The homeless, https://www.aa.com.tr/en/europe/invisible-owners-of-streets-and-squares-in-italy-the-homeless/2707816
13. Unesco (2022): Chile: Promoting the protection of Neurorights, https://en.unesco.org/courier/2022-1/chile-pioneering-protection-neurorights

14. Villalba, Enrique (2022): Parroquia de Santa Mónica: un icono artístico en Rivas https://www.diarioderivas.es/parroquia-santa-monica-rivas/
15. YouTube (2022) : Mes Aieux, https://www.youtube.com/watch?v=JvcEPoEjqIc
16. Schumacher, E.F. Small is beautiful. Vintage UK Random House, London, 1993

14. Toxic Ideology 6: The One World Government

1. Schwab, Klaus; Malleret, Thierry. COVID-19: The Great Reset (p. 219). Forum Publishing. Kindle Edition.
2. What it will take movements (2023): Why we need women to lead the global reset, https://whatwillittake.com/covid-gendered/no-3-why-we-need-women-to-lead-the-global-reset/
3. World Economic Forum (2023): Our Mission, https://www.weforum.org/about/world-economic-forum/
4. Heinrich Böll Stiftung (2023): The G7 and G20 in the Global Governance Landscape, https://www.boell.de/sites/default/files/uploads/2016/11/fundamentals2_eng.pdf
5. OpenAI (2024): Introducing ChatGPT, https://openai.com/blog/chatgpt
6. Harari, Yuval Noah: Sapiens: A brief History of Human Kind", Canada: Penguin Random House, 2017
7. IT World Canada (2023): Government of Canada to invest $30 million in AI in robots, https://www.itworldcanada.com/article/government-of-canada-to-invest-30-million-in-ai-in-robots/517756
8. European Commission (2023): The one billion euro brain, https://ec.europa.eu/research-and-innovation/en/horizon-magazine/one-billion-euro-brain

16. Freedom Of Expression: Our Most Powerful Tool Against Evil

1. The Heritage Foundation (2022): The Meaning Of The Constitution, https://www.heritage.org/political-process/report/the-meaning-the-constitution
2. CBS News (2022): Christianity in the U.S is quickly shrinking and may no longer be the majority religion within just a few decades, research finds,https://www.cbsnews.com/news/christianity-us-shrinking-pew-research/
3. CNN (2022): Elon Musk restores Donald Trump's Twitter account, https://edition.cnn.com/2022/11/19/business/twitter-musk-trump-reinstate/index.html

18. We Must Preserve Families At The Heart Of Our Civilization

1. Owens, Candace. Blackout: How Black America Can Make Its Second Escape from the Democrat Plantation (p. XIV). Threshold Editions. Kindle Edition
2. Europa ciudadana (2022): ¿Cuál es el perfil de la población, familias y hogares europeos?, https://www.europaciudadana.org/cual-es-el-perfil-de-la-poblacion-familias-y-hogares-europeos/

19. Education Is An Operation Of The Soul

1. Gatto, John Taylor. Weapons of Mass Instruction. New Society Publishers. Kindle Edition.2009
2. Statista (2023): Estimated number of homeless people in the United States from 2007 to 2022, https://www.statista.com/statistics/555795/estimated-number-of-homeless-people-in-the-us/

20. Education And Technology

1. Laje, Agustín: Generación Idiota: Una crítica al adolescentrismo. Harper Collins México, México: 2023
2. Ortega y Gasset, José: La rebelión de las masas. Barcelona: Ediciones Orbis, 1983

22. We Must Preserve Our Historical Heritage

1. Youtube (2023): Kamala Tries Explaining Russia-Ukraine Conflict,https://www.youtube.com/watch?v=_t7LqPWaJlo

23. The Kingdom Of God Is Within

1. Hawkins, David. El Poder frente a la fuerza: Los determinantes ocultos del comportamiento humano (Spanish Edition) . El grano de mostaza S.L.. Kindle Edition. 2014
2. Von Dreien, Bernardette: Christina, Zwillinge als Licht geboren. Deutschland: Govinda-Verlag, 2018

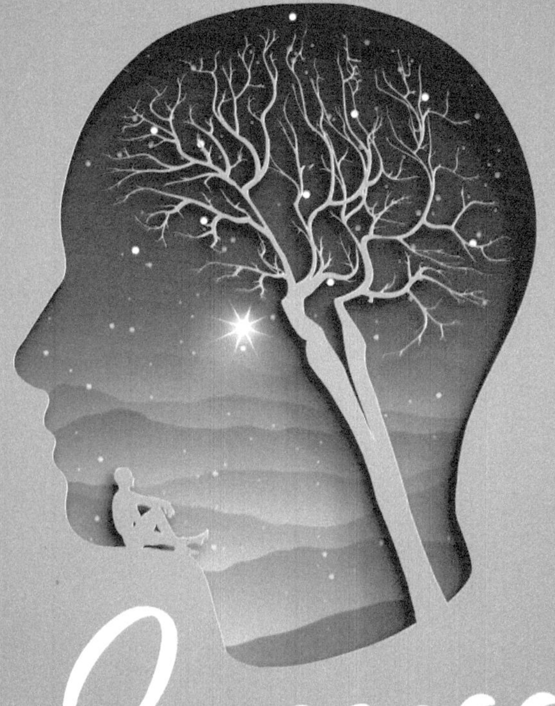

Take back the leadership of your mind

The Success MINDSET

Paola Knecht

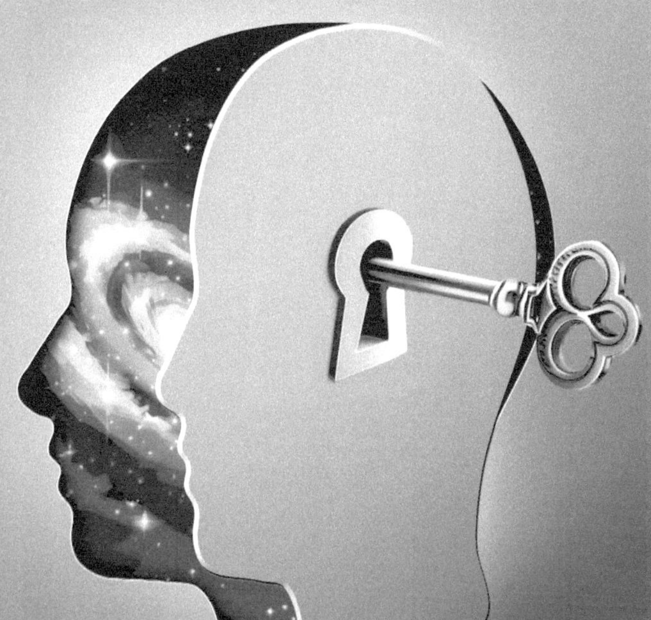

The Secrets OF DISCIPLINE

Paola Knecht